THE SAGE OF SAN DIEGO SAID CHOOSE QUALITY AND REASON

A New Enlightenment from The Western Tradition

Malcom Dalgliesh

A New Enlightenment, La Jolla, California and New York

To Truth Seeker James Hervey Johnson, and to Charles Smith, whose work and ideas made this possible. A grant from Johnson's savings, now partly in the J.H. Johnson Charitable Educational Trust, is acknowledged.

Published by A New Enlightenment,
P.O. Box 7024, New York, NY. 10128-0010

**The Sage of San Diego Said
Choose Quality and Reason:**
a socio-political critique of contemporary religions in a historical and evolutionary perspective.

ISBN 0-9646438-0-4

1. Religion - Christianity - Islam - Judaism - Marxism
 Egalitarianism - Equalism - circumcision - philosemitism-
Everlasting Life.
2. Sociology - welfare - foreign aid - ethnology - eugenics -
immigration.
3. Evolution - ethnic differences - racial differences -
heredity.

Contents

Cover photo credits Bob B. Yarbrough/Roving Eye, Eva Ops.

Our motto is carved in stone over the entrance to the Virginia State Archives in Richmond:

Reason and Free Inquiry are the effectual agents against error. They are the natural enemies of error and error only. – Thomas Jefferson.

James Hervey Johnson believed San Diego was the best place in the world.

Johnson introduced the papaya plant to San Diego, and lived to pick fruit from his own trees, supplementing his vegetarian diet. His intellectual colleague and philosophical heir, a descendant of the cousin of the philosopher Jean-Jacques Rousseau, introduces us to some of their Qualist philosophy and way of looking at the world, particularly the Western world.

These are related to contemporary issues, with samples of the moral and social confusion resulting from belief in Christian, Jewish, Mohammedan and other superstitions, and suppression of discussion.

The material is in the direct down-to-earth practical form of expression that Johnson preferred, with references from people, press, radio, TV and cinema. Radically centrist politically, the New Enlightenment world view truly gives evolutionary direction to improving the quality of life and meaning to the expression Everlasting Life.

Supportive letters and arguments from readers are invited. You will be eligible for complimentary copies of new developments of A New Enlightenment.

Published by A New Enlightenment., P.O. Box 7024, New York, NY 10128-0010 and La `Jolla, CA. 92037-7561.

A New Enlightenment

We are creating, storing and associating information of quantitative galactic magnitude, yet we live in a political environment of social confusion. Cybernetics allows us to produce manufactured products of improving utility, durability and quality, with decreasing cost and use of labor; agricultural productivity increases, but the numbers of poor and malnourished increases. The preserves of indigenous peoples, wild animals and plants are being squeezed smaller, yet world population increases at the highest rate in human history. We have more facts available to us than any generation before us; but there is more likelihood of being robbed, raped and killed in countries from Russia across Europe to North America, and much of the rest of the world, than there was in our parents' generation.

The reason is unreason. Vital data are misinterpreted through the software programs of universalistic religions and ideology, so that the data are wrongly computed or assessed and the answers to the most important issues are wrong. The effects of using wrong answers are socially disastrous, reducing the quality of life and of the arts, which are expressions of human life.

A *Weltanschauung* is a philosophy of life, a world outlook with views, creed, ideology, that prescribe thoughts and actions. The program of the annual meeting of the American Psychiatric Association for 1994 suggested that "a patient's world view provides a key to understanding the individual's self-image, interpersonal relationships, concepts of health and happiness, moral and spiritual values, and attitudes towards illness and death" (1994 Annual Meeting Information, p. 48).

Weltanshauungen, world views, come with the milk. They are absorbed from the family, the community and school, or clan, tribe, nation, and communications media. Being brought up as an Atheist, Christian, Communist, Egalitarian Humanist, Jew, Moslem, Buddhist, Ba'hai..., offers differing world views: views that may influence almost every thought and action for the rest of our lives. A religious fundamentalist is unlikely to disagree with that.

Does it matter whether political decisions that affect our present and future are based upon or are extensions of one of these world views? Undoubtedly, it does. Religion depends upon faith. It is analogic, metaphorical. Although the Enlightenment after Europe's wars of religion bore Western civilization the scientific method of inquiry and the great political method of separation of church – or non-rational belief, and state, in the last half-century we have slipped back.

This is why the Sage of San Diego, James Hervey Johnson, and his editorial predecessor, the Qualist American philosopher Charles Smith,* focused the greater part of their expression of belief and writing on exposing the evil of religious belief and the theology of Egalitarianism and its societal expressions. Egalitarianism, or as Smith called it – Equalism, is a faith and suppression of truth common to contemporary classical religious authorities and to the recent religion of Marxism and much of Humanism. By evil one means self-destructive, inimical to the continuation of diversity of species, inimical to Qualist concepts of "life everlasting."

The post-World War II rulers of the West have confirmed the answer to Friedrich Nietzsche's question: What has caused greater suffering than the follies of the compassionate? – It is not compassion, but the follies of faith that we want to stop.

The hope that the Enlightenment of Western Europe two hundred years ago would extend its liberation of mind and spirit from superstition, from using sacred texts and wishful thinking to guide public policy, rather than using rationalism, is unfulfilled. But "the people," our fellows, are generally unaware of this. Marxism masqueraded as rationalism, but enforced the dogmas of universalism. Disregarding realities such as heredity, whole upper, middle or intellectual classes were destroyed. Its "priests" prescribed reading from its sacred texts, it saints were Marx and Engels, Lenin, and later Mao. It had martyrs; and death for those who stood firm in its way. Its ideas of equalism nestled in Western religious institutions and ivory towers. From them, as from the money sources of political power, denial and irrationality are propagated as the norm. Religious fundamentalisms are resurgent.

Every year, multitudes of believers swarm to the Ka'aba in Mecca, to St. Peter's Square in Rome, to the Wailing Wall in Jerusalem. Every January, tens of thousands of people still march

---

* Charles Smith was not only imprisoned when demonstrating for evolution at the Scopes trial in 1925, but arrested at Newburg, New York, in the early 1960s when passing out Truth Seeker leaflets he had written denouncing equalist welfare policies that subsidized illegitimate births for those unable to care for themselves, a policy that he believed was counter-evolutionary.

through eastern Berlin to honor the memory of "two Communist martyrs," Rosa Luxemburg and Karl Liebnecht. Luxemburg was one of the founders of the German Communist Party, and a co-founder with Liebknecht of the Spartacus Bund in 1918. They were official heroes of the tyrannical German Democratic Republic and huge marches were organized each January in honor of these international or would-be transnational false prophets. The parade is now organized by the Party of Democratic Socialism, successor to the East German Communist Party. But millions of people think and act every day in conformity with Equalist dogmas that spread from Marxism, that are also resonant in church, synagogue and mosque.

Contemporary methodologies of persuasion have created a new hierarchy of influence over what we think and are led to believe. Reporters write and commentators air the views of interests that are inimical to our survival (*Who will tell the People: The betrayal of American democracy.* William Greider, Simon and Schuster 1992). Michael Crichton was denounced as politically incorrect, and called a Japan-basher and a racist, for writing his novel *Rising Sun*, about Japanese sophistication and multi-level thinking compared. with Western one- or two-dimensional systems. It was politically incorrect largely because it raised consciousness of a fallacy of globalism and equalism. "If it had been written about Jewish businessmen, it would never have seen the light of day," firmly declared the international establishment periodical, *The Economist.* Crichton's warning of increasing Japanese domination is dismissed as "anti-Japanese invective" and if "references to unbridled Japanese control over American institutions and scorn about American response are not enough to prove it, Mr. Crichton provides a bibliography of articles and books on the subject and an afterward in which he calls on America to heed the warning" (*The Economist* 22 F. 1992, 86). Kill the Messenger! Deride defenders!

Japan's World War II objectives were the ridding of the Far East of European colonialism and the establishment of a Greater East Asia Co-Prosperity Sphere. In spite of military defeat, these aims have been accomplished - and much more: the former European colonial powers and the USA and Canada are now deeply in debt to Japan. What an accomplishment! While the business press offers stories of the end of Japan Inc., researchers document Japan as the world's largest spender on civilian research and development

(Fingleton, E. *Blindside: Why Japan is Still on Track to Overtake the U.S. by the Year 2000*. Houghton Mifflin, 1995).

Japanese demonstrate their pride in themselves, unlike Western peoples generally. After the Kobe earthquake at the beginning of 1995, the Japanese Government declined Western aid. Foreign doctors were told they could not practice because they did not have Japanese licenses, and it was reported a month later that "A mountain of Tylenol still sits in a locked warehouse because officials expressed concern that it may not be appropriate for Japanese bodies" (*NYT* 5 F. 1995).

Free thought is the object of more powerful ideological attacks than at any time since the great conflicts between science and Christianity. The opposition of religious fundamentalists of all faiths to free inquiry and questioning – is resurgent. The danger they are to our peoples' present and future welfare joins the power of ideological equalists who have dominated all media in western countries for the last half-century, as well as the ivory towers of learning and their legislatures. Some hold that no differences are significant, some decry "verbal violence" and demand that no one give offense (*Kindly Inquisitors: The New Attack on Free Thought*. Rauch, J. Chicago Univ., 1993). But there is a growing and spreading awareness that this should change – that something is wrong, because we experience the deleterious effects of using these dogmas rather than truth. The light of reason that a precious few genuine freethinking atheists have held in the years of suppression is beginning to be seen by others.

We know where universalist religionists and transnationals, cosmopolitans and Marxists and most Humanists will generally stand on issues such as alien immigration. They are for it. Some have a religious conviction that poetic metaphors such as "the brotherhood of Man" are to be taken and used literally. Since use of poetic imagery as literal fact is likely to be as disastrous as setting out on a ship of the desert – a camel – equipped for a sea voyage, so the use of religious poetry and propagandist metaphors as our guide is resulting in the dissolution of Western civilization. Instead, we should use the best information available to us without prejudice, and make the best projections of the consequences of our actions and policies as part of our decision-making process.

Advancement of quality – of life, of individuals, of societies, of the environment, of the future – is more likely to occur if we use evolutionary and evolving reason and information, than if we grope in the darkness of religious supernatural belief and the sentimentality of modern Humanism and Equalism.

The intellectual development of the West for the last two centuries has been in the milieu of a European-American utopianism and universalism, provided by the Enlightenment, and a revival of Christian universalism. At the end of the twentieth century, we are also increasingly subjected to the amorphic globalism of transnational capitalism. It moves easily along the interstate highways built and maintained by Judeo-Christian universalism. Its power is so great that it may only be curbed by nation states. If these are not retained and manned by democracies of sufficient homogeneity to provide a common will, then a soft tyranny of centralized global "oligarchic collectivism" (Orwell *1984*) is highly probable.

Visit the town of Langres in eastern France, where Diderot was born the son of a cutler, who by the age of fifty was admired by the highest nobility, and best minds of Europe; the man who produced an encyclopedia of information up to his time. He was part of a movement of bringing information into the relations between peoples, patterns for power, and thinking about beliefs, which we call the Enlightenment. The *Encyclopedia* states that for the philosopher "civil society is, so to speak, a divinity on earth." The truth of his propositions is grounded in reason, proof, and observation.

Diderot and his contributors to the project of the *Encyclopedia* gave people access to information for independent judgment and collective action. He wrote "In time this work will assuredly produce a revolution in mens' minds, and I hope that all tyrants, oppressors, fanatics, and intolerants will be the losers thereby. We have served mankind..." (Diderot's *Lettres à Sophie Volland*, Gallimard).

Information now available to us exposes utopian-universalisms as an illusive mirage, not in harmony with the nature of Nature. They had their utility. Continuing to use them as social, cultural and economic goals dissipates the strength and character of western culture, and dilutes it by diversion into the global sea of mixed multiculturalism and whirlpools of confusion. The development of children into responsible adults is assisted by a sense of stability of the space they occupy and as clear a sense of ethno-cultural identity as possible.

Seeking unifying theories and forces that underly the physical world, a quest since ancient Greece, continues appropriately. Observations, theories, appraisals of systems underlying human diversity still challenge our capacity to understand their order.

A key to a positive future is the strengthening and evolution of cultural norms that are consistent with a world view that best fits the way nature really works. It should provide a way to a future that we prefer.

To live in harmony with other animals, plants, and even planetary topography, is an ideal toward which hopefully more and more of us will strive, and insist that our governments act to extend the ideal beyond our individual reach. But what of human harmony? How may we live in a greater degree of harmony between groups of people, of races, ethnic groups, tribes, nationalities? By dissipating western superstition with rational supportive life-enhancing alternatives; by replacing misinformation with the best information we have; by the strengthening and evolution of positive cultural norms. In western thought, were we to harmonize our world view towards reality as we can best understand it, this would release creative energy that could be expressed in a great increase in the quality of life and an epochal outpouring of positive arts.

Slip away from the thought police who guard the media and the mind; and leave the mediocre who are intellectually enslaved but do not know it, or do not care to know it. At the time of the last Enlightenment, John Milton wrote of them in *Paradise Regained* (Book iv, 143-5):

> *What wise and valiant man would seek to free*
> *These thus degenerate, by themselves enslav'd*
> *Or could of inward slaves make outward free?*

Let us reclaim Liberty of thought and expression of our understanding of reality. We shall experience a New Enlightenment.

This was the belief of the Sage of San Diego who opposed religion as against reason and quality. He was attacked and reviled for relating the philosophy of qualism and evolutionary reason to contemporary issues, exposing the analogic of religion. His offices burned down, and he noted in his Will that he might be murdered because of the expression of his views. This was not paranoid; for our ideas may provoke anger and hostility in those who feel threatened by them; threatened because they have invested part of themselves in untruth, and only the courageous can bear with grace the loss of part of themselves and their past in exchange for enlightenment. There are those who would move to suppress and vilify us for writing it.

Johnson and I understood that new ideas have to be processed through minds capable of responding to factual material. We have used recent factual material in this publication and placed it with historical perspective. But we both believed with Hippocrates that eventually "Whoever does not reach the capacity of common people and fails to make them listen misses the mark."

He asked that after his death I should carry on this work with the means he had worked most of his life to provide, and give it the widest distribution. This is one of my efforts to do so, the first using means he left for the purpose. But regrettably, the major part of those means has, so far, been put to other purposes. Such are too often the ways of trustees and lawyers – of whom Johnson never said a good word in my presence, quite the contrary.

We shall carry forward A New Enlightenment to the best of our ability for the benefit of our present and future. Superstition and suppression are our enemies. Join us.

2

A Civilization Self-destructs

Outside the British Museum in London is a notice: Please do not feed the pigeons. Why?

From the patristic age of Christianity to the followers of the socialist comte de St.-Simon (1760-1825), to the communes of Anabaptists, to the death camps of Jonestown and charismatics like Koresh in Waco, Texas, to the present, the "Marxist" principle of "from each according to his ability to each according to his need" has been in the Christian canon. The principle can be found articulated in Acts 4:32-35:

> Now the company of those who believed were of one heart and soul, and no one claimed that any of the things he possessed was his own, but they held everything in common....There was not a needy person among them, for as many as were possessors of lands sold them, and brought the proceeds of what was sold and laid it at the apostles' feet, and distribution was made to each according to his need.

Marxism (Karl Marx came from a rabbinical family), with its millenarian belief in a future of happiness and justice where all give according to their ability and receive according to their needs – and states have "withered away," with mainstream Christianity and Islam, supports the dissolution of biologically homogeneous societies. Their classification is Believer or Unbeliever. But ethnocentric, coherent systems of belief support the stability of a society. Belief systems can give comfort, fortifying us as individuals to sublimate sorrow, and accept pain. Societies can diffuse the burden of suffering by sharing it with a communion of friends and relatives, this comparing with expressed emotion in prayer to a savior, a saint, a prophet, a god. Homogeneous societies with generally shared systems of belief enjoy a complementary cohesion, and express themselves with generally acceptable institutions and unique cultural expressions.

Man is mostly a group-preferring animal. From mate to family, clan, tribe, ethnic group and largely homogeneous nation, self-identification includes part identification with a group. Birds of a feather flock together.

But many Western religious organizations, interpreting meta-phorical language such as "the Brotherhood of Man" in which "there is neither Greek nor Roman, Jew nor Gentile, circumcised or uncircumcised, we are all one in Christ Jesus," as literal, have a responsibility for Western confusion. Religion is older than reason; analogy is older than logic. It is a form of art, a system of metaphors. (Smith, C. *Sensism: The Philosophy of the West.* New York: Truthseeker. Vol. II, 1019) Further, the religionists are unwitting functionaries in the creation of a New World Order of mixed-up peoples and centralized power. For the centralization of world power is not only the objective of competing pope (Martin, M. *The Keys of This Blood.* 1990), prelates, and ayatollahs. Their efforts for ethnic dissolution should be welcome means to an oligarchic money Establishment behind the core promoters of a "global plantation," behind the Bilderberger Group and the Trilateral Commission. Christians, perhaps all religionists, with religion as their raison d'être, are politically naive and politically vulnerable, good subjects for political manipulation.

Rights affirmed in the Bill of Rights of England's "Glorious Revolution" of 1688-9, (that also declared the illegality of the Ecclesiastical Commission Court), and reflected in America's Bill of Rights, were immunities against government intrusion into personal and community relationships. With leadership and intense support of "Reverends" of seemingly all denominations and "Faiths," what so-called "civil rights" legislation has done is to abrogate the rights of individuals and communities, allowing federal judges to dictate how many low income homes must be built in a community, or how many children of what color must be sent to schools outside it or brought in, or how many people of what gender or race an employer must choose. And we must be very careful in choosing the words we speak and the emphasis, for prosecution, fines, and loss of employment will result if it is judged to be even politically incorrect, insensitive, let alone "hate speech." Spurious guilts and psychological traumas are inflicted on children as education, and reinforced in general media messages. With "doublethink," legislation has divided and disintegrated communities in the name of integration.

The process of "social engineering," using legislation and sanctions to enforce it, has consumed immeasurable resources of ability and energy, of time and money. They have been dissipated and their positive employment diverted. To offer a very small example: the state of Missouri had to spend nearly $1,000,000,000 up to the beginning of 1995 in desegregation "battles" with Kansas City, to satisfy several Federal court orders, which required them not just to desegregate the schools, but to elevate the achievement level of the students. But problems arising from the presence of children of ethnic minorities in schools are found across America, Europe, Australia, and elsewhere modeled on the "integration" and assimilation that are supposed to be the American model. Yet at the same time, there is a growing understanding of the "evil" of past white American attempts to .integrate and de-tribalize and erase American Indians, or "Native Americans," as a distinct people.

But no one else calls the social engineers to account for the losses. We do.

Previous generations had coherent systems of ideas to explain their world and what happened in it. In the dawn of eighteenth century Enlightenment, Puritan preacher Cotton Mather of Boston wrote in his diary after his daughter was badly burned in a household accident, "Alas for my sin, the just God throwes my Child into the fire!" This was consistent with a much-quoted essay *BONIFACIUS: Upon the Good* he had written in 1710. Cotton Mather was a learned man with a library of nearly 4,000 books, who later gave an extensive explanation of Newton's physics in his book, *Christian Philosophy*. It was an attempt to integrate new facts and philosophy, evidence and faith.

A revolutionary change of thought was taking place among European peoples in the 17th century. What had been thought to be divine authority was being replaced among intellectual elites by results of observation, experience and experiment.

Rationality and this scientific method, and genius, have given us at the end of the 20th century technological and information revelations or revolutions. The faith of Cotton Mather may seem far from most of us today, but inappropriate "Alas for my sin" still exists for many Christians and those of other faiths and non-objective world views. Moreover, the group altruism that is a part of the sociobiological system – useful for the survival of a homogenous group, is now politically manipulated to the detriment of peoples, and Christianity is a common accomplice.

In 1980 Wausau, Wisconsin, best known for the insurance company that is based there, was Norman Rockwell midwest. The census that year showed it to be the most homogeneous, whitest city in the nation. Its 32,000 people felt safe, crime was rare, with jobs for everyone. All friendliness, godliness – and generous. In the mid-70s, when Wausau's heart was touched by the plight of southeast Asian refugees, and a local church invited a few families to come, everyone felt good.

A local doctor remembers that when they first came to town he thought, "That's kinda neat. We're actually going to have somebody in town besides a white German or a Pole. By the same token, I had no idea of the situation ahead of us."

What happened is that the refugee population ballooned to over 4,000 in just over a decade. The first immigrants sponsored their relatives, and they in turn sponsored others. Now they are eleven percent of the population. Culturally, they could not be more different from the good burghers of Wausau. Seventy-five percent of the immigrants are on public assistance. Very few pay local taxes, and Wausau is feeling somewhat less generous.

"We've given and given and given, you know," says a local leader, "It's time for them to give something back. The numbers are so high now, I think that's part of our insecurity. What shall we do? The jobs haven't increased and the people keep coming."

Almost all are Hmong, a nomadic, agrarian people from the highlands of Laos, refugees from Nixon and mainly his national security adviser Henry Kissengers's "secret war" in Indochina, when Central Intelligence Agency employees bribed thousands of hill tribesmen in Laos to try to block the Ho Chi Minh supply trail into South Vietnam, an effort that proved to be futile.

They may lack technical skills, they have customs that seem primitive to Wausau natives but they have a perfect understanding how public assistance works, and they know that Uncle Sam never misses a payday.

A Hmong leader says: "When my family came here in 1975 we were the very first group. They were sponsored by American families. Now immigrants are sponsored by Hmong. Now they have a militant Asian minority. You think we are not going to be here in the next century," she says. It would be natural if they, perhaps like other non-white minorities, look forward to a time when they will be the majority and, with a one-person one-vote formula, displace those whose language and culture are now dominant.

Is that what the people of Wausau intended? Of course not. But their religion and the value system associated with it that persists and is reinforced in a Marxist-influenced media, still inhibits them from self-understanding and makes them impotent to assert themselves. White Wausau still wants the education they pay for to teach the history and culture which is their heritage. The Hmong want the same thing for themselves – their history, and their language. A hard reality were the increased property taxes as more large Hmong families of eight, even ten children came to school, increases of as much as ten percent a year. They tend to live in the same neighborhood, making Wausau liable to penalties for de facto racially segregated schools. Busing children far from their homes had to be instituted to avoid legal penalties. A situation once unthinkable in this once-homogeneous community of 32,000. A school board that voted for busing was replaced by the electors. A former member admits to white flight from parts of town and a movement to send white children to private schools, some because they felt their children would be held back by being with slower Hmong-speaking children. Parents complain of gangs in the schools and that Wausau had its first drive-by shooting between Hmong and Laotian teenagers in an area where once they took evening walks as their children rode their bicycles.

"To the people who have lived in Wausau all their lives it was a rude introduction to our brave new world." So said a commentator on this true Wausau story, told on CBS TV in a 1994 60 Minutes Magazine broadcast.

"Wausau is being penalized for being good," says a community leader. Communities round Wausau have not made Asians feel welcome, so refugee immigrants come to Wausau. "Thanks to federal law and post-Vietnam guilt syndrome, the immigrants keep coming," said the TV commentator, "there are thousands more in the camps in Thailand." When he said, "What you are saying is that if these people would just get up and go away, this town would be a great town again," a group of Wausau whites gasped and said "Oh no! Not at all" and so on, expostulating, protesting and taken aback at the suggestion that such an idea would even occur to them.

They were protesting that they were not heretics. For at the end of the 20th century it is heretical in Europe and North America to believe that one would rather live in an unmixed racial society. And yet, of course, the same people may hold and voice the belief that the native peoples of the Amazon rain forests should not have to accept non-native immigrants into their living spaces, people who will destroy their habitats and way of life. This is self-deluding, self-destructive, Orwellian "doublethink." What these Wausau Christians have done is disrupt and disintegrate their community and jeopardize a future for their descendants in their Western tradition.

What the Hmong are trying to do, perhaps instinctively, is to recreate a new Hmong community – the more Hmong, the greater the potential for its achievement.

Klaus and Gisela Pfleger, a retired German couple on vacation in California, were photographing spring flowers on a scenic hillside in May 1994 when three Hmong young men walked up to them, shot them in the head and drove away with Mrs. Pfleger's purse. The woman was killed and her husband seriously injured. The father of one of the killers said, "Back in our country, you never saw things like this happen. There are no thieves, although our houses are not as nice as here. Nothing would come into your house except for the animals you own."

"We have lost all control," a father of one of the murderers said. "Our children do not respect us. When my wife and I try to tell my son about Hmong culture, he tells me people here are different, and he will not listen to me."

Largely at the instigation of church groups in the "sanctuary" movement and the guilt-ridden, more than 100,000 Hmong tribes people have been brought to the United States, beginning in 1980. They are a clan-based people whose culture centered on slash-and-burn farming and had no written language until recent times.

From the first years after their arrival, the Hmong's culture brought them into conflict with American law because some engaged in the medicinal use of opium, the kidnapping of brides or the ritual slaughter of animals. A few have leaped the cultural divide, but most remain alienated.

The Hmong were used as the American Indians were used in the French and Indian wars two and a half centuries before. Christians who worked so hard to bless these people with American citizenship are so primitive in their appreciation of cultural differences and human ecology. The same is true of people who adopt children of another race and culture. Gene Roddenberry's Prime Directive in the Star Trek television series has more wisdom. Additionally, it often seems that the degree of failure of American interventions in the affairs of other states is directly proportional to the number of subsequent immigrant-refugees into the U.S.A. from the area of conflict.

The future development of quality of life of the peoples of Western countries – and their lands and plants and animals – are threatened qualitatively and quantitatively by non-Western immigration, that Christian universalist dogma welcomes and the globalist establishment and its media bars warning against.

In California in 1994, "illegal immigration was the all-encompassing issue. It helped re-elect Gov. Pete Wilson, declared down and out just a year before by pollsters and pundits. It swept Proposition 187 into law, cutting off schooling and non emergency health and public services to illegal immigrants....On a sunny Sunday in October more than 70,000 opponents of the initiative marched in Los Angeles waving Mexican flags left over from the World Cup. Live TV coverage brought the rally into living rooms across the state. Participants and observers felt the tide was turning.

"But at anti-187 headquarters outside San Francisco, campaign professionals cringed. 'We didn't want them to march,' said Dick Woodward, a veteran Republican political consultant who ran the campaign against the initiative. As city crews cleaned up after the demonstration, private pollsters measured public opinion. In the days after the rally, support for Proposition 187 sky-rocketed while opposition cratered" (*NYT.* 27 N. 94). The majority had unintentionally been given a glimpse of a future and rejected it. Woodward seems to be a mercenary with talents for sale, a role of ancient lineage in European societies. But the mercenary with access to the mass media is as powerful an enemy as was once the condottiere with sword for hire or the password for the keepers of the city gate.

There is such confusion of religion, race, and culture. The Wausau story is an example of what James Hervey Johnson, the Sage of San Diego, called Christinsanity. Similar stories can be told about other immigrants in every country of Western Europe and North America. With present trends and no change in relevant policies, in a few years indigenous Britons will be a minority in several London boroughs, and almost a minority in others. The future of many major cities from there to America's Pacific northwest is similar. Seattle's population is already 12 percent Asian, 10 percent African-American, and 3 percent Hispanic. Vancouver, British Columbia, is 30 percent Asian – largely due to immigration from Hong Kong – is poised to become a city with a majority of "minorities."

The guides for a new enlightenment are to be found in what we already know of anthropology, ecology, ethology, evolution, sociology and so on. Is there an analogy between the introduction of the Hmong pair into the supportive Wausau community and the introduction of a pair of rabbits into Australia? The suggestion may seem outrageous to some people. But the analogy is in the introduction of a breeding pair into an area without the controls on proliferation in their original habitat. That habitat for the Hmong, including competition for food and short life expectation, compares with a paradise of natural resources made available to them without the effort of accumulation and storage in Wausau.

A similar system applied in Britain after World War II. There, where "cradle-to-the grave" welfare systems and programs of "full employment" were introduced to honor pledges made during the war that their "working" lower classes would not return to the same social conditions of large-scale unemployment, malnutrition, and poor housing that existed before the War with Germany, where these conditions had been largely eliminated in less than a decade. For the peoples of India, Africa, and the West Indies, to be provided with child allowances, free medical services, old age pensions and so on without ever having had to contribute anything towards them was an incomprehensible miracle. "Go to England Baba," a young Indian accompanying an expedition to Everest was heard to tell an old disabled man in the foothills of the Himalayas, "there they give you money for nothing."

Is it any wonder that there are now millions of non-Europeans in Europe? Large and increasing areas of Europe are alienated from it. Since a country's institutions are products of their people and history, indigenous institutions are often unsatisfactory for the cuckoo-colonists. But, to take England for example, Britons are polite and diffident when the neo-colonists who are displacing them tell them they are "racist" and that their institutions are oppressive.

"They do not even seem to mind writing out multiple-zero welfare checks for penurious immigrants, with their multifarious needs – and governments no doubt find it easier to go with the universalist flow than to risk censure from 'the international community' by enforcing the stricter immigration controls, or pursuing the monoculturalist programs, that are now necessary if Britain is to retain something of its immemorial character. Government ministers, senior civil servants, academics and intellectuals have been affected just as much as the middle classes by the universalist, chiliastic philosophies and vague feelings of racial collective guilt that have made these demographic changes possible.

"Few could have foreseen what would follow in the wake of the trickle of relatively well-educated [by British colonialists] West Indians and Asians that started in 1945; to them Britain was so strong and so close that they could not conceive of its dissolution. Impossibly cultivated and well-educated by today's standards, the war generation could not have imagined a situation when most Britons, even academics, would regard their own culture as worthless, or let the insane fallacies of deconstructivism, moral relativism, pluralism, equality and Afrocentrism pass almost unchallenged" (Turner, D. *Chronicles.* Jan. 1995, 38). There were some, with vision, who did, like Enoch Powell, but these Noahs who warned of the flood were ridiculed and vilified by the controllers of the media. Their very names were made anathema.

The churches in England may be emptying, but it is the residual Christian and international socialist milieu that made its people vulnerable to the paralytic sickness of pseudo-guilt. They are like AIDS sufferers, their defenses, their immune systems, attacked and reduced by the Christian strain of the virus of equalism. The infection has racked the body politic since the Second World War, and its immune systems are daily weakened by toxic media input. (The British experience is described by Goulbourne, H. in *Ethnicity and Nationalism in Post-Imperial Britain.* Cambridge: Harvard Univ. Press, 1991.)

There is a parallel between population growth in certain non-industrialized countries, officiously termed Less Developed Countries, and growth of Aid to Families with Dependent Children (AFDC) in the U.S.A., that supports aid to poor mainly single mothers – some of them having two children before the age of twenty, as their mothers did – in the last 40 years. The number of children receiving AFDC increased from some 2 million in 1950 to over 9 million in the early 1990s. The world population grew from 2.5 billion in 1950 to over 5.3 billion in the early 1990s. This represents a transformation of labor, of natural resources, of plants, animals, money – into people!

This growth has been largely funded by taxing Western workers with small or no families. Internationally, this transfer of their earnings has been carried out via foreign aid, the International Monetary Fund, the World Bank, unrepaid international bank loans, A.I.D., and hundreds of small tax-exempt agencies based in Europe and the U.S.A. The transfer of wealth has occurred from Western Europe and the U.S.A. and Canada. Even in the U.S.S.R., families with large numbers of children in some eastern republics such as Uzbekistan, were subsidized by workers in the western republics, many with self-limited families averaging under two children. The total wealth that has been transferred from Western workers to others as "aid" since World War II is probably comparable to their entire national debts. Is this rational?

These facts are results of human intervention, or human engineering, of global proportions and significance. Where upward social mobility is possible, and the reproduction of those at the bottom of the socio-economic pyramid is subsidized, the relative number of those least able to care for themselves increases. This is not the way nature works.

Promoting, supporting these regressive policies, and tacitly suppressing criticism of them is the religious-equalist coalition and their secretive Big Brother, the transnational oligarchic supra-capitalists.

European countries still spend substantial portions of their workers' and taxpayers' money on overseas welfare and development instead of using it to help the neocolonists and their children return to their former habitats. For Europe is a comparatively small area with enough of its own people for a good cultural life, with heavy tasks of restoring areas of ecological abuse to use, leisure and beauty. Germany, with the largest ecological problems, the largest loss of territory from World War II but the largest immigrant population, has a pilot project showing what could be done on a larger scale, and by the other countries of the European Union – probably the most important joint project for the development and welfare of their peoples. We look for it to appear on more party pledges.

On 11 January 1995 Germany and Vietnam agreed that Germany could begin to return thousands of Vietnamese, almost all of them former contract laborers brought to eastern Germany by the government of the former German Democratic Republic. At the same time, Germany pledged development aid equivalent to about $6.5 million annually, including funds for re-integration programs for returning Vietnamese. Bonn also pledged to expand existing government export guarantees for trade with Vietnam, and said that it would "encourage" German firms to invest there. Advocacy of policies of repatriation is not "extremism," as the supra-capitalists, transnationalists and socialists use their media to trumpet, as in France, with 6 million African neo-colonists. This is a program for happier peoples with less frictions in more stable political societies.

As long as potential colonist-immigrants are seduced by an easier life without economic incentives to return, the less likely the younger ones are to want to return. But there are, for example, Chinese, who are returning to China from the U.S.A. to participate in and to have their children be a part of the great future they believe is ahead for that country. Is that a combination of patriotism and profit?

"The vast majority of conservative Christians," writes William Bennett, want nothing more than "...safe streets, good schools, strong families, non-intrusive government and communities where people care for one another" (William J. Bennett, *Credit the Christian Right*). Yet these are the same people who act as the Christians of Wausau acted. Further, while they may talk of non-intrusive government, many conservative Christians have a goal of overturning *Roe versus Wade* and so depriving women of the choice as to whether or not they should bear a child with all the responsibilities that decision brings. (One's world view and circumstances should be the critical factors in deciding for or against abortion. The societal problem is that the more responsible and foresighted people are more likely to take up the abortion option in this society, and these are valuable personality traits with a probable genetic component.) Fundamentalists may play down their religious agendas in statements to the press, highlighting issues such as low taxes and pro-business policies, but many would also deprive children of the insights provided by Darwinian observation and hypothesis and Sociobiology. If we use these insights and inculcate them in our children, the beauty and benefits of ethnic diversity may survive, without them it is improbable.

European Christians now meld late-20th century universalism of the church with the concept of removal of frontiers between states. Open-border Christians like Bennett, denouncing California Proposition 187, reconcile their American identity with universalism by believing that "the American national identity is based on a creed, on a set of principles and ideas." This is not true.

The idea and practice of *E Pluribus Unum* was never intended to apply to non-Europeans. It is only since the post-Kennedy flood of non-European immigrants, and African-American assertions of their own heritage, that multiculturalism has become a leading national issue. There are parallel situations in all Western countries. In his draft of the Declaration of Independence, Thomas Jefferson referred to a homogeneous people "of a common blood." The first congressional statute on naturalization in 1790 restricted American citizenship to "any alien, being a free white person." Jefferson at first believed that the American Constitution would bring American-style republicanism wherever it was introduced. But long before his death he had the evidence of its failure to do so in many new states, and he recognized that its cultural origin and utility went together. The federal immigration code restricted immigration on the basis of "national origin" until 1965, intentionally favored the continuation of European immigration. The law's repeal was made possible by denying that this would significantly alter the ethnic and racial composition of the United States. It was a flagrant deception.

There is more than comfort and safety where there is a commonalty of ethnicity, culture, interest (Brubaker, R. *Citizenship and Nationhood in France and Germany*. Cambridge: Harvard Univ. Press. 1991). The misunderstood example of the U.S.A., the metaphorical melting pot of Europeans, misled Europe to the contemporary treatment of the state as only a territorial organization. **Western survival now depends upon refocus on the neglected view of the state as a membership organization, as an association of citizens with a commonalty of ethnicity, culture, interest,** a rational concept of utility that recommends itself. Further, a state of unrelated individuals or mixed races or unacculturated ethnics must be authoritarian (cf. Singapore) or chaotic, "for democracy implies the acceptance of majority decisions, and this in turn presupposes homogeneity – in the sense that the minorities identify themselves with the whole sufficiently to place the interests of the whole above their own" (Ritchie, R. *Enoch Powell 1992.* 1989, 145).

The laws of a viable democracy are part of the institutional structure that expresses common values, and a commonalty of world view. Great Britain gives us the example of an increasingly disparate society necessitating radical changes in the spirit of the laws and the dimensions of civil liberty for the new society to function. An editorial in the *New York Times* (27 F. 1995, A 14), is headlined "British Justice, No Longer a Beacon." It criticizes a new crime law, "The Criminal Justice and Public Order Act," as "a dangerous retreat for a nation that pioneered the concept of individual legal rights, but has in recent years steadily eroded those rights....The already parlous state of civil liberties in Britain is going to get worse. There is a cautionary lesson in that for the United States...." What is the lesson?

Britain's Christian culture sacrificed freedom of speech and other liberties won centuries ago in exchange for racial harmony. But the disparities of culture and history in the new British multicultural society, that they believed had worked for America, are breaking it apart. More restrictive laws are needed to hold it together, for society to function.

From its inception, Christianity has put its followers under the tension between a personal religion, calling upon each person for a personal conversion: "Daughter, thy faith hath made thee whole" (Mark 5:34); and a communal religion dependent upon a church: "Thou art Peter, and upon this rock I will build my church" (Matt. 16:18); "That they may be one, even as we are one" (John 17:22). It is more than wishful thinking for there to be a perception that nearly all the papal social encyclicals for example, beginning with Leo XIII's *Rerum Novarum*, have sought a middle path between "all things are common," and "not for the rich to appropriate an undue share," in the words of Clement of Alexandria.

There are other religions that recognize our dual nature anthropologically as having characteristics of communal herding animals, but also in varying degrees and at various times, of more or less solitary ones. Man is generally a group-preferring animal. From mate to family, clan, tribe, ethnic group and largely homogeneous nation, self-identification includes part identification with a group. John Locke held that one could legitimately remove resources from Nature's common stock, but only where "there (was) enough and as good left in common for others." Garrett Hardin has reviewed the concept for our time in his eminent essay, *The Tragedy of the Commons* (Science, 1968, Vol. 162. 124-138). But there is also self-assertion: "The ego posits itself. I am, is an act."—Nietzsche.

At the true center is the third way. It lies between exclusive individualism and religious or plutocratic transnational globalism. It includes individualism in a context of group loyalty and group altruism. These are a basis of what used to be called civic virtue. It is undermined and destroyed by an influx of strangers who take advantage of the supports available for the common good of the community (herd), exploiting them for their advantage, for example in breeding numbers, over the existing community. This is what has happened in Wausau, across Europe and America at an increasing pace over the last half century, and continues at this moment.

If Christians understand this, can there be a meeting place between evolutionary qualists and Christians who can double-think to support survival of human diversity? For though we may hope to convince "all Men" to join us, it is not rational to expect it. For many are moved by other factors than reason, and all of us are possibly vulnerable to them at some time in our lives.

Those who can clear themselves from the cobwebs of superstition, and false inculcations of childhood or media, those who think rationally of an evolutionary present and future, may possess a new Enlightenment. Like all humans except sociopaths, and some animals, the people of Wausau, Wisconsin, exhibit altruism – like other traits – in varying degree. Altruism is of evolutionary value by enhancing the probability of group and gene survival. When altruism is projected outside the group and applied universally, the effect is likely to be negative to survival of the group. Suppression of dissent and criticism against paying for community services and "welfare" for those outside the group, affirmative action, foreign aid, assisted immigration, are in this negative category of Western behavior. Its sickening effects on the body politic, on civilized discourse, on quality of life of most Western peoples is apparent.

James Hervey Johnson acted altruistically during his lifetime towards defending and securing the future of his group. For the same reason, we are devoting our time and ourselves to writing this elucidation. For your people, your group, their future is in your power too. Depend upon it.

3

Islam

A revolutionary change of thought was taking place among European peoples in the 17th century. What had been thought to be divine authority was being replaced among intellectual elites by observation, experience and experiment. The death and destruction of the Reformation and Counter-Reformation, culminating in the horrors of the Thirty Years War from 1618 to 1648, were largely over. The war drew in nearly every power in Europe. In destruction of people in central Europe, it was comparable to the Black Death in the 14th century. But Queen Elizabeth of England, who died in 1603, had allowed the practice of Roman Catholicism, provided Catholics did not plot against her crown. Henry IV of France, after defeating Spain, signed the Edict of Nantes in 1598, allowing the Huguenots to worship in their fashion. William Shakespeare and Jean-Baptiste Molière created characters influenced by superstition and others free from it; and Shakespeare showed how "signs and portents," and the entrails of animals, had once been subjects of belief or disbelief for heroes of history like Julius Caesar.

Shakespeare was now free to write of man: "How noble in Reason! how infinite in faculty! in form, in moving, how express and admirable! in action how like an angel! in apprehension how like a god."

John Milton's seventeenth century epic, Paradise Lost, informs the ages on free debate:

> Though all the winds of doctrine were let loose to play upon the earth, so Truth be in the field, we do injuriously by licensing and prohibiting to misdoubt her strength. Let her and Falsehood grapple; who ever knew Truth put to the worse, in a free and open encounter.

The social utility of religious toleration was becoming acceptable, but could still be challenged.

The people of Vienna with 10,000 soldiers and unprepared defenses were nearly overrun by a great Turkish army numbering 200,000 in 1683. Vienna and Europe were saved from the fate of Constantinople by the arrival of a mixed army of mostly Germans, Austrians and Poles commanded by John Sobieski, King of Poland. Islam's last great threat of military conquest and replacement of European with Levantine civilization was removed in 1697 by the brilliant experienced general, Prince Eugene (or Eugen) of Savoy commanding the Austrian army, and young Elector (Kurfürst, "Blau") Max Emanuel (1670-1726) of Bavaria. But without these men and the sacrifices of those who served with them, the increasing light in Europe would have been put out, and we should not forget them.

As we may listen today to a wonderful recording of the Viennese organist Martin Haselböck playing the Toccata No. 5 of Johann Kerll on the 1636 fest organ in the Klosterneuberg Monastery (Novalis CD-150094), we can remember that his family, like so many others in the towns and countryside around Vienna, were sent to Turkey as slaves for work and use for sexual gratification, while anguished Kerll shared the fate of Vienna, besieged for seven months. Had Vienna fallen, there would be no music of Kerll, no organ or place to hear it - and no organist!

The music of Johann Sebastian Bach, Handel, Mozart, Haydn, celebrates the period of transition of theistic culture to one in which the secular was predominant. Without Sobieski and Eugen and the men under their command, the churches and palaces where these musicians played and where their songs and music may still be heard today, would not have been created. The effect upon us of the transformation of Vienna and the heart of Europe into a Moslem center had it fallen to the Turks can hardly be imagined.*

In France, a temporary regression was the Revocation of the Edict of Nantes. The Edict had allowed toleration of Protestantism. With the Moslem threat to Vienna relieved in 1683 by forces he had rallied, Pope Innocent XI saw in the Revocation at Fontainebleau in 1685, a new unity for France and Roman Catholicism,

---

* Would we be here today if Charles Martel (called "The Hammer,") and the Franks had not stopped the conquest of France by the Saracens at Tours and Poitiers in 732? If the Golden Horde of Mongols, one of the most devastating military organizations the world has ever seen, had not turned back from making mountains of European skulls in the 13th century, because of the death of their great Khan?

Edward Gibbon speculated two centuries ago of an alternative future had Martel's victory not occurred:

"A victorious line of march had been prolonged above a thousand miles from the rock of Gibraltar to the banks of the Loire; the repetition of an equal space would have carried the Saracens to the confines of Poland and the Highlands of Scotland: The Rhine is not more impassable than the Nile or the Euphrates, and the Arabian fleet might have sailed without a naval combat into the mouth of the Thames. Perhaps the interpretation of the Koran would now be taught in the schools of Oxford, and her pupils might demonstrate to a circumcised people the sanctity and truth of the revelation of Mahomet" (*The Decline and Fall of the Roman Empire,* vol. vi.,15).

(Bibliography *Les Huguenots*, Paris: Archives Nationales, 1985) that sent a small remnant of Huguenot survivors from the bloody atrocities of the siege of Rochelle, the Protestant stronghold on the west coast of France, to New York to found New Rochelle in 1688, the year before England's "Glorious [because bloodless] Revolution."

The history of the British people and their North American colonists has never seen the fires or smelled the smoke of the great armies of Islam. Unlike the peoples of southeastern Europe, they have never had their prepubescent girls and boys taken from them to serve their Moslem masters in harems, or as Janissaries against their own people.

The British people of our time were astonished by the demonstrations in the streets of London after Salman Rusdie, a writer born in India but living in London, was sentenced to death in February 1989 for blasphemy in *The Satanic Verses*, a book he had written, by the Moslem cleric Ayatollah Ruhollah Khomeini in Iran. Thousands of people of an alien culture suddenly occupied the streets of central London, calling for Rusdie's death.

A visitor saw "thousands of clenched fists punch the air in Parliament Square, outside the 'Mother of Parliaments'…and pondered the arrogant placarded messages: 'Islam – Today Our Religion, Tomorrow Your Religion.' The indigenes were clearly in retreat on all fronts…" (*Chronicles*. Letter From London. Jan. 1995, 38).

Living too long in London, yet writing from a posture of Asian Third Worldliness, a denouncer of "white prejudice" in Europeans who defended their heritage, Rushdie was presumably unaware of his fading understanding of what was happening at his cultural roots. He had "evolved," as the French used to say of apparently Europeanized colonial subjects; often people who had passed through the Sorbonne and emerged as Marxist intellectuals, useless for anything but revolution.

He not only applied the skeptical European tradition to a religion that still takes itself seriously; he quite forgot that in Qum and Islamabad there are people who just can't take a joke at all. And so the man who believed that he stood for Them – the oppressed of the Third World – found his life threatened by Them, while he was guarded by Us, with our "old colonial attitudes," bred of 400 years of conquest and looting.

Inevitably, he tried to deny the implications of this. While defending himself and his book, he insisted that "I have never seen this controversy as a struggle between the Western freedoms and Eastern unfreedom." This was the equivalent of Dreyfus's *"Vive l'Armée!"* But Rushdie, like Dreyfus, was wrong. Whether Dreyfus liked it or not, his case was indeed a conflict between two cultures and two sets of values. Our own Affair over *The Satanic Verses* is similarly a *Kulturkampf* between two opposed sets of values, whether Rushdie likes it or not or knows it or not (*Atlantic Monthly,* March 1994, 43).

Even in the United States, the constitutional "wall of separation" of church and state has constantly to be defended from certain Christian fundamentalist groups, and from Jewish zealots in support of Israel and state kosher-labeling laws (Frankel, M. *Faith and Freedom.* 1994). In India, separation of church and state in the Western sense was understood by Jawaharlal Nehru, India's founding Prime Minister. Nehru's western secularism died with him. Thereafter politicians openly displayed their religiosity. Official functions began with prayers, and ministers sought advice from astrologers and had tantric rites performed to insure success. India may retain a secular facade but an increasing number of government officials, intellectuals and journalists talk the language of Hindu fundamentalism, protesting that religious minorities merit militant repression. From their point of view, they are presumably reasserting traditional community attitudes, national and moral (Juergensmeyer, M. *Religious Nationalism Confronts the Secular State.* Berkeley: Univ. of California Press, 1993). Islamic, Christian and Jewish theocrats would return us to pre-Enlightenment intolerance, when toleration of dissent was toleration of evil, – which was evil.

Rusdie had picked up a contemporary Western illusion, expressed in part by the belief that religious-cultural differences are no longer of any significance or consequence. From World War II until now, it has been politically unacceptable or "incorrect" to suggest the existence of a *kulturkampf*, a competition of cultures in the *global village*. The struggle is occasionally seen on the surface – a controversy in France over girls coming veiled to school, or over toleration of genital mutilation of some African girls according to their family tradition (partial or total labiectomy and clitoridectomy, also infundibulation). Perhaps now that economic regionalism is growing, the fact of a competition of cultures can no longer be excluded from discourse: "On the other hand, economic regionalism may succeed only when it is rooted in a common civilization. The European Community rests on the shared foundation of European culture and Western Christianity," opined Samuel P. Huntington, professor of government at Harvard University, director of the Olin Institute for Strategic Studies, in *Foreign Affairs* (Summer, 1993). This contention is evident at the margins of the European Community, for example. Turkey, with a predominantly Turkic Asian people of Moslem tradition, living in a land where Greek, Roman and Byzantine artifacts speak of the Turkish conquest of the territory; and Israel, where an Ashenazic, Khazar or East European elite wish to claim a European market inclusion for a Near/Middle Eastern country and people, where only Jews are allowed a myth-based exclusive "right of return." (Ashkenazic Jews are mainly of converted Khazar stock. Khazaria was in the northern Crimea area. See *Archeology*, March/April 1992, 6.)

Mosques, of course, are mushrooming all over the western world, except in former Yugoslavia, where to Serbs and Croats they represent centuries of Turkish colonial rule, loss of land, a differentially increasing Moslem population, and a history at least at times, of severe religious and political repression. Yet the strengthening of Islamic fundamentalism and acts which others call terrorism, may be attributed to Western politicians' cowardice and hypocrisy, and media partiality. (There are an estimated 7 million Moslems in the United States, and increasing numbers of Moslem immigrants in the old industrial towns of Europe, e.g., 27,000 in Glasgow.) There are 2½ million Moslem settlers in Germany, with about 20 mosques, the largest at Mannheim, built in 1995. Some perspective maybe gained by imagining Turkish reaction to a similar number of German colonists and new churches in Turkey.**

In a report "Bosnia to Beirut" he edited, Robert Fisk, a British correspondent in the Middle East for *The Independent* for

---

** Germany has virtually no non-European colonial past and has maintained its traditional conception of rights of citizenship based upon *jus sanguinis* - citizenship by descent. In spite of naturalizing about 70,000 non-Germans every year since the 1980s, German governments are under intense pressure from internationalists within and without the republic to make their country irrevocably "multicultural," or of mixed race and nationality. Yet Germany has had over a third of its pre-World War II territory confiscated by the victors, with over 12 million Germans driven from their homes and lands. This was the greatest dispossession of a people in history.

seventeen years, concentrated on American policy's partiality for Israel at the expense of the Palestinians. Only Islam seems to oppose their oppression with force. "For them Zionism is an abomination, the occupation a cruel insult, America the Great Satan and murderer, even of civilians, and Islam a road to paradise." (A production of Chameleon Television for The Discovery Channel, *N.Y. Times*, 27 Ap. 1994 C18:4-6. An account of some attempts to parry Zionism's U.S. lobbying is given by Paul Findley, congressman from Illinois for 22 years, in *They Dare to Speak Out*, (Westport: Hill, 1985). Sen. William Fulbright, chairman of the Sen. Foreign Relations Committee for many years, was not re-elected after complaining in the Senate "Here we are voting $50 million for schools and hospitals in Israel, and I can't get $7 million for roads in Arkansas," and saying on Sunday television that 80 per cent of the Senate would vote anything for Israel.)

Can one compare the power of the idea of Islam with firepower of Western weaponry? Impervious to western intimidation or material incentives, the Iranian theocracy affirmed Rusdie's death sentence five years later: "The sentence has to be carried out irrespective of whether the apostate repents or not."

An observant Moslem living in an Islamic fundamentalist society, conforms in a seamless civilization, one where science and faith, philosophy and religion, all speak in unison. When a young Moslem comes to America to study, the experience is unsettling. Our lives seem full of dissonance and contradiction. Above all, there is the baffling, seemingly compartmentalized role of religion in the lives of all but the most devout westerners. The Moslem thinks that everything that people do in the West is related to their religion, in the same way that everything he was doing back in the Islamic world was related to his religion. He cannot understand that there are many people here for whom the basis of their action, the criteria which determine the value of their action, the morality or lack thereof, has very little to do with their religion - even if they hold onto a religion. He cannot understand the category of a secular mind. First there is individual behavior - social, sexual, which we associate with individual choice, but which a Muslim might assume is expressing religious dictates.

One has seen the culture shock with some young members of diplomatic staffs when they come to their missions to the United Nations Organization in New York without prior western exposure.

If a woman allows herself to be alone with them, it implies that she is open to sexual intercourse. Conversely, young western women who have met students from Islamic countries at universities, and have the narrow vision of equalism or so-called universalism, may be severely shocked to find that in the land of their husbands, they may never be able to leave home alone.

"But there is more than loose morals and a secular, popularized culture." At George Washington University in Washington D.C., where more than a thousand students are Moslem, many of whom he advises, Dr. Sayyed Nasser says. "Islam is concerned equally, if not more, about your high culture - its intellectual assumptions and traditions." These too, he says, are jarring to the newcomer. The first thing is that there seem to be so many voices that are contradictory and without some unity. There is the voice of modern science, the voice of sociology, and the voices of the humanities, and there is very little relation between them - and within those contexts, there are so many different theories and points of view presented that the non-western student finds it very difficult to orient himself intellectually.

Like pre-Renaissance Christianity, Islam believes that all Art is related to some function of life. A visit to an art museum may therefore be an unsettling experience. The idea that a Renaissance altarpiece is not displayed to be venerated but admired, is alien. To depict an infant Jesus on his mother's lap is a disturbing image to Moslem eyes. It is an example of the humanization of these religious figures, and therefore a detraction. (Dr.Sayyed Hossein Nasser is the author of *A Young Muslim's Guide to the Modern World,* a theologian and professor at George Washington University in Washington D.C., where he advises many of the Moslem students.)

(Observant Judaism also proscribes figurative human, animal or other representation as potentially idolatrous.)

What the foreign student and the native may never find out is that there is an alternative secular relatively coherent view of the world. The student is separated from it by a "glass" wall. It is almost invisible. You may only see it if you have been shown where it is. A few find it by hitting it or seeing others hit it and getting hurt. On the contrary, Western – particularly American college campuses, are used by fundamentalists to proselytize. (The activity is funded by the potentates of Saudi Arabia, Kuwait, and the Gulf Emirates, American "allies," some of whom have in the 1990s flogged women for inadequate veiling in public, and carry out sentences on their subjects like Rusdie's. London's *Daily Telegraph*, reported 4 S. 92, p.11. "A Shi'ite was beheaded yesterday in eastern Saudi Arabia for blasphemy and renouncing the faith, officials said.")

Fundamentalist Islam gives the feeling of strength, of certainty, to its followers. Those who fought battles against them in previous centuries knew its weight and at certain times and places it was faced by equal zeal of those who believed they fought for Christ, Christendom, and the only true faith. Fundamentalist Islam provides inspiration for the dispossessed and oppressed Palestinians, for example.

In Gaza, a generation that in the United States might be led to idolize some raw musician or vapid athlete hyped by the media seems to idolize the gunmen and suicide bombers of the Islamic Holy War against Zionism and its supporters and products. Their pictures hang in homes and on key chains. Walls are covered with graffiti saluting them and with bold drawings of their attacks. At some demonstrations, young men wear shroud-like sheets, showing their readiness to die in the Jihad.

Such respect for "holy death" was resurrected in the late 1980s, when the Palestinian Childrens Uprising or Intifada began, and many children took part in or witnessed street clashes with Israeli soldiers. Hisham Hamad, a suicide bomber from Islamic Holy War who killed three Israeli soldiers in the Gaza Strip in November 1994, wrote in his Will or testimony: "The life of this world is just a game and an accumulation of possessions and children. What God has is better for me than all this. I am to leave you, but let me meet God. I love paradise more than this world."

The bombers have typically been devout young single men who experienced personal loss or humiliation at the hands of the Israelis. "It is an act of ultimate control," said Dr. Iyad Sarraj. For a person otherwise impotent compared with the Israelis, "You control death, you control life, you control your environment and you decide when to die."

"We don't call this suicide, which is forbidden in Islam," said Imad Falouji, publisher of a Hamas newspaper. "These are martyrdom operations. We are commanded to wage holy war for the sake of God. Here the attacker is assured success, he avoids arrest, inflicts heavier casualties on the enemy and gains martyrdom."

But Dr. Mustafa al-Masri, a psychiatrist at Gaza's only community mental health program, says there is a depression in his country. "At social gatherings you hear people talking about basic needs, political and economic problems, but there is no mention whatever of the future. In the hopelessness and helplessness of this world, there is the bright promise of the next life" (*NYT*. 25 Ja. 1995).

Fundamentalist Islam has been strengthened and is strengthened by American political and military intervention, tilting and favoritism in the relations between Near and Middle eastern states. For the military power of the United States can only be matched by the power of the spirit of "holy war."

Islamic scholars may insist that "jihad" does not always mean holy war or even "war" in the Koran. Some traditionalists believe that the "great jihad" is the battle within one's self to live in accordance with God's will. But in the overcrowded streets of Middle East cities, quotations from the Koran, like quotations from "holy" writings elsewhere and throughout human history, are substitutes for rational thought and factual knowledge. Just as there are otherwise well-educated people brought up in the Christian tradition, for example, who do not wish to free themselves from its prejudices but reject Christian fundamentalism and zealotry, so there are such "moderates" in Islam. The Egyptian, Tunisian and Algerian Governments use broadcasts and newspaper space to differentiate between the hues of the Islamic spectrum of ideology. Judge Sayid al-Ashmaway, who lives with bodyguards and rarely leaves home, is Egypt's most prominent critic of militant zealotry. His books are required reading in many schools in Egypt and elsewhere. "The Islamic mind is confused," he said. "People do not understand the proper definitions of Islamic terms, but believe the distorted definitions. Religion has become mixed up with politics and out of this has come an ideology. This militant doctrine must be replaced by a liberal Islamic doctrine."

The separation of mosque and state, and the secularization of politics, was a process which had begun in the Middle East. It was seen in the nationalist movements in Egypt, Syria, Iraq and Algeria, for example. It should have led to increasing enlightenment of their people and a falling away of the bonds of superstition and its fears. Relative impotence of Middle Eastern states compared with the power of interventionist states – America, and to a much lesser extent Britain and France – in that order, have aborted the process of those states secularization and enlightenment. For only the "true believer," carrying his bomb or driving the explosive-filled van to suicide and paradise, may use death to overcome the might of the "Great Satan," the enemy of his people.

Was it the blast of American bombs dropped in the Middle East that was felt as the World Trade Center in New York shook in 1993?

4

Judaism and Philosemitism

Writing in *Commentary*, a periodical founded by the American Jewish Committee, the socialist-turned-conservative, or neo-con, Irving Kristol, called on American Jews to recognize that American Protestant fundamentalists are "strongly pro-Israel." Excusing an evangelical leader who said that God does not hear the prayers of Jews, Kristol wrote: "Why should Jews care about the theology of a fundamentalist preacher?... What do such theological abstractions matter as against the mundane fact that the same preacher is "vigorously pro-Israel?" (Kristol, I. "The Political Dilemma of American Jews." *Commentary*, Vol. 78, July 1984, pp. 24-5). *Commentary's* editor, Norman Podhoretz, broke with liberals in the 1970s when he came to realize that "continued America support for Israel depended upon continued American involvement in international affairs, from which it followed that an American withdrawal into [neutrality] represented a direct threat to the security of Israel." (Ginsberg, B. *The Fatal Embrace*, 1993, 204).

Two decades later, a member of a younger generation of neo-cons was asked if there might be conflict between conservatives and the Christian Right. "I don't see Pat Robertson [a fundamentalist former presidential candidate and founder of the 1.5 million-member Christian Coalition] as being opposed to Jewish interests," Jay Lefkowitz responded. "Deep down, I believe that a little anti-Semitism is a good thing for the Jews – reminds us who we are. Such views serve a useful purpose. They remind Jews of their identity - which is especially important in an era when the threat to Judaism from anti-Semitism pales in comparison to the threat of assimilation" (*NYT Magazine*. 12 F. 1995, 65 and 5 Mr. 1995, 12).

This thinking gives non-Jews an insight into Jewish thought and action. For Irving Kristol, "the typical New York-Jewish view of the world [is] that people who weren't from New York and Jewish were unfortunate: they ate Wonder bread and mayonnaise and had boring existences" (*NYT Magazine* . 12 F. 1995, 38). The simplest level of meaning or understanding of these statements is that they are expressions of feeling by unassimilated ethnics with a degree of grandiosity. To those working for a new enlightenment, in evolutionary perspective the behavior is an expression of group altruism. "Is it good for the Jews?" as a criterion for evaluating policies and options, optimizes the probability of group survival.

In the nineteenth century, a minority of immigrant Irish organized to influence policies of the United States of America so that Ireland would be favored or Britain opposed. Before World War I, Jacob Schiff, a Jewish investment banker in New York, tried to get President Taft to raise tariffs on Russian imports until the Russian government removed certain restrictions on Jewish activities. This is what the Jackson-Vanik amendment did in our own time. Some African-Americans from time to time choose or promote foreign policies that they believe will help African peoples. These are consequences of being "a nation of immigrants" and of some immigrants remaining invested in ethnic or racial loyalties.

Jewish identity and separation are reinforced by the ethno-religion of Judaism. It may be called an ethno-religious centrism. Parallel conditions exist for certain other immigrant groups, but because other groups are much less influential, their impact on the general society is usually much less or limited to single issues.

But why are Jews more influential? Can their history offer insight? A Christian minister who visited a Jewish village in eastern Poland before World War II came away with an impression of squalor, but a disgust with a people who were always figuring out deals, "even with possessions amounting to two goats," as he said. On the other hand, they were forever talking and arguing, and had high regard for Talmudic disputation, which ranked with wealth in their selection of spouses for the children. These are characteristics of a contemporary American society that Jews have worked hard to form according to these predilections. Their significant place in the 20th century history of promotion of non-figurative art may be a result of Judaism's censure of representational art. The implications for a people "sans arts plastiques," were speculated upon by the philosopher Ernest Renan in his 5-volume *History of Israel* (1887-94). He was dismissed from the faculty of the Collège de France by Christians after stating that Jesus was "an incomparable man."

The consequences of many centuries of Jewish genetic selection of certain traits for reproduction, could be part of classroom teaching on its effects. They could be compared with the probable effect of centuries of idealization of celibacy promoted by the Christian Roman Catholic church, and followed for generations by some of Europe's most intelligent men and women. But for this, one has to accept the evidence for the importance of heredity in intellect and accomplishment.

Jews are strongly represented in important national and

international American societal activities and relationships, and certain of their organizations' policies reflect fear that this issue may become part of public discourse, questioned openly, and then opposed. This is Jewish realism, for it has happened before in the history of Jews and the places where they "have achieved enormous status, wealth and power, only to be cast down, driven out –or worse." (Ginsberg, B. op. cit., ix). The exercise of power from positions of privilege by ethnic outsiders characteristically and historically produced varying degrees of antagonism and aversion or revolt. Now, as insurance, frequent polls are taken to test the possible rise of public feeling against them.

At a meeting some years ago of the American Society for the Scientific Study of Religion, a Dr. Glock presented his findings on gentile attitudes towards Jews in the United States. At that meeting, a representative of the Jewish Anti-Defamation League of B'nai Brith (ADL) complained that although his organization had financed the study, it offered no insight into the causes of what is often mislabeled "anti-Semitism" in America. What the ADL finds to be an enigma has an explicable basis. Namely, that non-Jews may feel resentment or other expressed emotions at the influence that Jewish representation makes possible, a perception that an ethnic group that may be five percent of the American population, is forcefully over-represented in many aspects of American society. Secondly, that this group makes decisions on a basis exemplified by the quotation from Irving Kristol. Would this insight help the representative of the ADL? A San Francisco court found the ADL guilty in 1993 of keeping dossiers on private citizens, using their own investigators and police contacts.

At an annual meeting of the American Political Science Association in the late 1960s, a symposium on factors in the formation of American foreign policy was moderated by Karl W. Deutsch, a political scientist born in Prague, who had left in 1938 and made a name for himself at Yale and Harvard. During the discussion period, he was asked if there was not a Zionist lobby which sought to influence American Middle East policy. Deutsch curtly swept the question aside with the put-down that this was "part of the conspiracy theory of history," not worth considering. Only in the *New York Times* of 8 August 1975, did David Binder's article, headlined "The Israeli Lobby in Washington is Small and Effective," make it possible to mention an Israeli lobby without risking boycott by being immediately labeled "anti-Semitic." Deutsch was later honored by the government of the Federal Republic of Germany. A book, *The Lobby*, by Jewish journalist Edward Tivnan, has since been written (Simon and Schuster, 1987), and a leading correspondent of The *New York Times*, Thomas Friedman, has recorded that it has justifiably been "considered the most powerful lobby in Washington" (5 Nov. 1992, A24).

In Hollywood and the American entertainment or communications industry, that have increasingly come to represent much of the idea of America to the American people and the rest of the world at the end of the twentieth century, "minority" control or predominance is generally recognized. The contemporary equivalent of Napoleon's saying "the pen is mightier than the sword," is "the entertainment-information power is mightier than military-industrial power," for "communications" influence the funding and use of military power. The locus of qualitative communications power, the direction and control of that power, should therefore be the concern to everyone everywhere. But whenever this is written up, the author and his publisher are at risk to be stigmatized with the "AS" word.

Neal Gabler clearly demonstrated in his acclaimed book, *An Empire of Their Own, How the Jews Invented Hollywood*, how the early Jewish movie pioneers such as Louis B. Mayer and Irving Thalberg (Fitzgerald's model for *The Last Tycoon*) who founded the studios of today came to Hollywood and "simply created a new country – one where they would not only be admitted, but would govern as well." (It was often an America idealized and personified in male and female characters that they envied, and used, in the case of female stars sexually, when they could.)

"And govern they always have," wrote William Cash in *The Spectator* (29 Oct. 1994). "That every studio head is Jewish today is no different from 60 years ago. 'Of 85 names engaged in production,' a 1936 survey noted, '53 are Jews. And the Jewish advantage holds in prestige as well as numbers.' In a recent *Premiere* magazine 'Special Power Issue' – ranking the 100 most powerful people in the 'Industry' – the top twelve were Jewish. There were no black or British industry executives ranked."

Cash also quotes George Steiner's saying that to be Jewish is to be a member of a club from which you cannot resign. He records that "In Hollywood, the most obvious examples of the Jewish Club are in the side-shows, the lawyers, talent agencies and management and production offices." "Experts," spokespersons, and key media people, are very often Club members. These are examples of ethnic networking. Alan Bellow, the son of novelist Saul Bellow, says Irving Kristol is "a great maker of connections," describing how he was inducted by Kristol into the neo-con counter-counterculture. At a meal at the American Enterprise Institute, where he has elegant offices, an article in the *New York Times Magazine* describes Kristol coming over and asking his son William, "'What's the name of our Jew from the West Coast?' (Answer: Dennis Prager, described as 'a not-so-right-wing Rush Limbaugh' who has a popular call-in show in Los Angeles.)" (*NYT Magazine*. 12 F. 1995, 61, 37).

Cash quotes Walter Isaacson, Time Inc.'s media editor, according to whom the old White Anglo-Saxon Protestant hegemony was linked through shared educational (i.e., "class") bonds and beliefs. "What binds these guys is a sense of interlocking ventures and relationships. The Old Establishment was a club. The New Establishment is a network;" its leading members the Titans of Tripe, as Auberon Waugh called them.

Other ethnic groups also network, giving their business whenever they can to their own people, for example. It is an example of the "birds-of-a-feather" fact of natural life. What is exceptional about the Jewish example, is the contrast between their relative numbers and their influence upon critical sectors of public life. This may produce questioning and criticism. It has, as noted before, historical antecedents. For example, when Hjalmar Greely Schacht, U.S.-born former president of the Reichsbank, was questioned by an Allied denazification tribunal at the end of World War II, he said that he had never been a National Socialist German Workers' Party member, but he had questioned the fact that Jewish people, with their own unique history and religion, exercised such a major control over Germany's cultural outlets. Is it Anti-Semitic (AS) to record this? The Sage of San Diego believed that the influence touched upon here has produced a distortion in the development of Western culture.

Predictably, Cash's article, inspired by the founding of a new multibillion dollar studio by Steven Spielberg, record billionaire David Geffen and their "best friend," former chief of Disney Studios Jeffrey Katzenberg, was tarred in the *New York Times* with quotes that called it AS. Cash's editor at Britain's *Spectator* was asked why he had published the article, with the innuendo questioning whether Cash should still be employed. The editor replied that while he was Jewish, he did not see the article as being more than observation. (Incidentally, what this "entertainment" complex may represent is a reassertion of the Club in a leadership position, after Japanese buying into the industry.)[*]

It is in this environmental system that the film *Schindler's List*, based on a novel by an artful Australian Irishman, was first projected on a screen in Germany. There had been more than half a year of media preparation and investment in hyperbole. On 1 March 1994, 800 people – Germans and Jews, diplomats and artists and film makers – "came solemnly together in the municipal theater under the patronage of President Richard von Weizsäcker to see the German premiere of an American film many Germans thought one of their own should have made long ago: 'Schindler's List' by Steven Spielberg."

"The reactions at the end were tears, stunned silence and a

---

[*] William Cash's analysis points toward two further insights.

1. Identity. The pioneer generation of Hollywood moguls reached for an Anglo-Saxon identity or ideal in many, now classic films of the 1930s, as Ralph Lauren seeks to do with his contemporary "Polo" fashion productions. Louis Mayer attempted to live like a 19-century aristocrat and even toyed with the idea of converting to Catholicism. Now, "Bill Stadiem, a Harvard-educated former Wall Street lawyer who is now a screenwriter in L.A. told me that he recently came across an old friend there who had been president of the Porcellian at Harvard - the most exclusive undergraduate dining club. His friend - a would-be producer - was dressed in a black nylon track suit and had gold chains on his wrist; dangling around his neck was a chunky Star of David. Stadiem asked, 'Why the hell are you dressed like that?' The Wasp replied, 'I'm trying to look Jewish.'"

2. Trophy women. Cash describes Birgit, a glamorous blue-eyed blonde, "her father, who owns one of Hitler's pianos, is German, told me that when she worked as a personal assistant to Vic Sutton, the Jewish head of the fast-track LA commercial talent agency, Sutton, Barth & Vennari, her boss would often - if signing a deal - bluntly ask if they were Jewish. 'I was surprised,' she said. 'I mean, in England, you'd never hear someone ask, Are you Anglican? On the other hand, he liked to boast that he had this hot young Nazi working for him. When I told him my family flew in the Luftwaffe he was ecstatic.'" She was a trophy. Offspring of an former oppressor, she was now his to obey, to command. A similar dynamic may exist in an African and white relationship, for example. The slave's descendant now commands, owns a daughter of a slave-master. Anthropologically, the ultimate destruction of an enemy is the abduction and or neutralization of its females, ending its possibility for breeding. This is a dynamic with powerful emotional content that may be difficult for the new "master" to control.

smattering of applause that was cut short as if somehow out of place. 'It needed you to do it,' Mr. von Weizsäcker told Mr. Spielberg when the lights came up.... Each guest was asked to donate 100 marks, about $60, to a German charity called Against Forgetting to restore a deteriorating memorial at the former Nazi concentration camp at Auschwitz" (*NYT* 15 Mr. 1994).

The holocaust story has been imbued, saturated, with a religious type of emotion where non-believers or questioners of Holy writ are kept outside the new Pale of decent society. The viewers of the projections of *Schindler's List*, with titillating scenes of nudity and sexual sadism to embed its content deep in the psyche below reason, had experienced a new type of church service with minister Spielberg!

With saturation of the media around the screening of *Schindler's List*, further restrictive legislation was passed in the Bundestag. On 26 April 1994 the Federal Constitutional Court announced that denial of the Holocaust is a "Provenly untrue assertion; propagating that assertion constitutes a punishable offense."

And with the film's worldwide exposure, *The New York Times* Thursday, March 9, 1994, boldly headlined *A First for the U.N.: Condemning Anti-Semitism.* "GENEVA, March 9 – For the first time, a United Nations organization condemned anti-Semitism today as a violation of human rights."

> In a broad resolution condemning abuses, the Human Rights Commission expressed concern that 'racism, racial discrimination, anti-Semitism, xenophobia, and related intolerance, as well as acts of racial violence, persist and are even growing in magnitude, continually assuming new forms.'

The forces of suppression and oppression had put their bait into the club sandwich. This was not subjected to any ballot in a participating country, and was certainly not part of a national agenda. It was an abortion of liberty supervised by the unelected who represented the U.S.A.

> The commission's decision to include anti-Semitism in its investigation comes three years after a successful American-led campaign resulted in the repeal of the General Assembly of a 1975 resolution equating Zionism with racism.

> But the vote today also means the United Nations has waited 49 years to decide that anti-Semitism is a violation of human rights, even though the human rights provisions of its founding charter were

heavily influenced by American and Allied horror at the Nazis 'final solution' in World War II.

Schindler's List did the trick. In liberty to challenge and criticize, we are back to Trotsky, Lenin and Stalin, and the Communists who ruled Eastern Europe after World War II, declaring anti-Semitism a crime and counter-revolutionary, as part of their establishment of power with control. In an interview published in the Communist *Daily World* (14 Jan. 1961), "Mrs. Hilde Benjamin, Minister of Justice of the German Democratic Republic since 1953, pointed out that anti-Semitism in any form was specifically outlawed in the GDR." As it had been as a first order by the Bolsheviks. Many people were imprisoned and killed on this charge.

In *A Concise Encyclopedia of Russia*, the editor S.V. Utechin, born and educated in the USSR, wrote, "The Soviet Government has formally always considered anti-Semitism as a relic of the past, and active anti-Semitism is treated as a crime. On the popular level an increase in anti-Semitism was noticeable towards the end of the 1920s because of the prevalence of Jews among the Communist officials" (New York: Dutton. 1964. 24).

So in 1994, in the so-called United Nations system, a new category of international offense was created, with which almost anyone could be charged. President Bush was denounced as an anti-Semite by high Israeli government officials when, as president, he temporarily held up a $10 billion loan guarantee to Israel to build new housing there.

Alfred Lilienthal documented in *What Price Israel* (Chicago: Regnery, 1953) and *The Zionist Connection* (N. Y.: Dodd, Mead, 1979) how the United Nations Organization is manipulated by promises and pressure. In the latter, he also illustrated the bias in reporting Israeli versus Arab news in the *New York Times* and that book publishers are also one-sided in their presentation. As I.F. Stone expressed it in "Confessions of a Jewish Dissident," his controversial article for *The New York Review of Books*, "finding an American publishing house willing to publish a book which departs from the standard Israeli line is about as easy as selling a thoughtful exposition of atheism to the *Osservatore Romano* in Vatican City."

In the state of illusion and advertising created by a motion picture, the first cantor to sing at the Vatican and the first person to sing in Hebrew there, performed on 7 April 1994. It was part of a concert for Holocaust Remembrance Day. "To perform in Hebrew with an Italian Christian choir at the Vatican with the Pope and 150 survivors of the holocaust in attendance was truly overwhelming," the cantor said.

Besides Germany, Belgium also introduced similar holocaust legislation following the showing of Schindler's List, and in France, Canada, Sweden, and other countries, questioning the presentations of the holocaust has been criminalized. In the United States, with freedom of speech as part of the Constitution, this has not so far been possible: but as a questioner, the future of your job or business will be in doubt. Anyone involved in business will almost certainly be aware of Jewish concerns, from paying to pass kosher inspection for their products, that can then bear identifying symbols on their labels, to doing business with or employing anyone who may criticize Jewish versions of the Holocaust, or Israel.

In 1994 an official of Japan's largest political party wrote a book urging politicians to adopt the political campaign tactics of Hitler. Hitler pioneered the use of aircraft to travel to and to be seen and heard by the people of many towns in Germany, supported by radio and advertising integrated campaigns. Although the book in no way described or suggested the adoption of Hitler's political policies, it was denounced by Zionist leaders. Probably because it extracted something positive from his experience. Similarly, when the February 1995 issue of *Marco Polo*, a Japanese conservative magazine, carried an article questioning the authenticity of accounts of the death of millions of Jews in homicidal gas chambers, rather than a much smaller number of deaths due largely to typhus epidemics and malnutrition – inevitable with Allied bombing of German roads and rail links, "the Weisenthal Center called on advertisers in *Marco Polo* to cease doing business with the magazine, Volkswagen, Mitsubishi Motors, Cartier and Philip Morris agreed to stop advertising in the Magazine, Rabbi Cooper [associate dean of the Center in Los Angeles] said" (*NYT.* 31 Ja. 1995. A11).

Marco Polo was owned by one of Japan's best-known publishers, Bungei Shunju. It announced that it would cease publication of the monthly general interest magazine which it said had a circulation of about 200,000. "All the editors and workers of Bungei Shungu accept the responsibility for publishing the biased article," Tadashi Saito, an assistant to the president at the publishing company said in an interview. He said the article showed "the low understanding among Japanese about the Jewish people and the Nazi camps." Face-saving, Mr. Saito said *Marco Polo* was three years old and not yet profitable. The threat to Japanese trade to the West had been erased. What is censorship compared with trading profits of billions of dollars at the end of the twentieth century? Money is the might that makes right.

In Paris, Japanese fashion designer Rei Kawakubo was forced to apologize to the European Jewish Congress. The Congress had denounced Kawakubo's display of striped pajamas in her Paris fashion show the same day the liberation of Auschwitz concentration camp was being remembered in Poland. The pajamas, it was said, were too reminiscent of the concentration camp uniform. Was the purpose of the vast process of "re-education" of Germany to inspire propagation of the light of the torch of Liberty from America? Or was the purpose to neutralize Germans psychologically with a burden of guilt? Or to suppress any criticism of Jews or Israel by calling it anti-Semitism, and equating AS with mass murder? Yet, in accordance with the Orwellian formula, people would believe that they were free. Goethe's dictum that the slave most difficult to free is he who does not know he is a slave, fits the German people of this period – and not only Germans. Liberty is having an equivalent of the First Amendment to the American Constitution written into the constitution of the Federal Republic of Germany, instead, it has always been restrictive of free speech – under the device of "protection of the constitution." The gag resolution in the Bundestag was pure *1984* in 1994.

Liberty is having an electorate informed about the means of public manipulation. In 1994 Steffen Heitmann, Justice Minister in the eastern German state of Saxony, for the first time came up against the invisible "glass wall" of political censorship which has been impressed upon Germany, and found his nomination to become Germany's next president withdrawn. "'We thought it was now finally possible to speak freely, but that was an illusion,' Mr. Heitmann said. 'There are rules about what can and cannot be said, and though these are not written down or even discussed, they are very strict. Certain subjects have to be treated in a very particular way. I violated these rules on several occasions, and I'm glad I did. I see a great difference between what you would call political correctness and what people really think. The gap is growing and I find that disturbing and dangerous'" (*NYT.*, 19 Jan. 1994, A:4).

A year later, 6,000 copies of a German translation of a book were destroyed by the publisher, after threats and complaints that it would support anti-Semitism, although written by a courageous Jewish researcher. The book, *An Eye for An Eye,* by John Sack (Basic Books, 1993), gives evidence that Stalin deliberately chose Jews to oversee secret police activities in the former German territories given to Poland by the Allies at the wartime Yalta conference. His conclusions were based on interviews with several high-ranking Jewish members of the Office of State Security, the Polish Communist Organization. These interviews gave evidence that, under Soviet supervision, Jews actually ruled and maintained some former German concentration camps in Poland after World War II, as death and torture camps for German prisoners of war.

Of course, there is "freedom of the press" in the United States. But James Bacque could not get published in the U.S.A. his detailed investigation into the deliberate policy of mass killing by starvation and exposure, of Germans in some French and American prisoner-of-war camps after World War II. It was published eventually in Canada (*Other Losses,* 1989). I have met an American guard at such a camp and heard him testify that this was true of the camp at Andernach, where he was on duty.

Nahum Goldmann, a man with nine passports and one of the worlds foremost Zionist figures, founder of the Conference of Presidents of Major Jewish Organizations and for many years president of the World Jewish Congress, the chief devisor and negotiator of the pact pledging West Germany to pay reparations to Israel and to individual Jews for acts committed during the Nazi years, lived mostly in Paris and died in Bad Reichenhall, Germany, in 1982. Before his death he created consternation by calling upon Israel to stop the savage bombardment of Lebanon's capital, Beirut. (Israel was using its heaviest American artillery.) He said the siege should be ended and official recognition given to the Palestine Liberation Organization. This position was immediately repudiated by the executive committee of the World Jewish Congress. Goldmann was fluent in French, and in December 1979 *Paris Match* published an interview in which he said that as a result of the climate of opinion created by the Holocaust, since the Second World War Jews have been treated *"avec gants de soie"* – "with silk gloves....Without Auschwitz, there would be no Israel." He knew as well as anyone how it had been used to obtain access to the taxes of the German and American people, and in increasing support or non-interference internationally whatever might be done in the name of Jewry or Israel under the beatifying halo of the Holocaust.

In *The Jewish Paradox,* perhaps in Paris, after a lifetime of Jewish activism, Goldman wrote, "You are a really impossible people, the most egocentric in the world! For every Jewish citizen arrested, somebody demanded my signature on a petition. Can you imagine something like that for the two million victims in Biafra, or the sufferers in Bangladesh. Does every single Jew have some God-given right to call upon the world's lovers of justice?"

In 1933 he left Germany, it was said, four days before the Gestapo came to arrest him for calling for a world boycott of Germany and its products, as long as it had a National Socialist government. He well understood the power of economic boycott. It was this experience that he carried with him when he negotiated reparations from the heads of the German and Austrian governments after the Second World War.

> The obtaining of German reparations after the war was, for me, one of my crucial successes. After being thrown out of Germany by Adolf Hitler, I returned to speak to [West German Chancellor] Konrad Adenauer almost as an equal. How these talks proceeded is a long story, and perhaps the one I am most attached to. I believe I have said that culturally I was still very German, at the same time as being a Jew and, in the 'universal' sense, a cosmopolitan.

The agreement that Goldman negotiated was a premium that Germany would pay with a lump sum and regular dues for the lifting of the trade boycott that Jewish organizations had imposed since 1933. Volkswagens, or the former German Chancellor's Peoples' Car, could now be driven unchallenged on American roads, and Germany could re-enter the markets of the Western hemisphere.

Another great success for Jewish organizations that impacts upon us all has been the adoption of "holocaust studies" as part of the curricula of the range of educational institutions in the Euro-American part of the world where their influence is strongest.

"Three episodes in the post-war years began to fix Israeli attention on the Holocaust, and Mr. Segev traces them in fascinating detail: the negotiations with West Germany, for general reparations and personal compensation, beginning in 1951, the so-called Kastner affair of 1954 (which referred to the failed deal with Adolf Eichmann, attempted by Rudolph, the head of the Rescue

Committee in Hungary, to trade one million Jews in 1944 for 10,000 trucks); and the trial in Jerusalem of Eichmann himself in 1960-61. Each of these occasions helped to raise the nation's slumbering historical consciousness, and to excite some reflections on the well-intentioned but misguided efforts to make pioneers of the future out of human beings who had not recovered from the memories of their ruined past.... The Eichmann trial in particular became a kind of national group therapy, as well as a forum for educating Israel's youth about the Holocaust" (*NYT Book Review* of *The Seventh Million*. Segev, T. Hill & Wang.).

There is also a dismissive review of another book which contains an essay by the well-known German historian of fascism Ernst Nolte, "who had an international reputation to lose," first published in the *Frankfurter Allgemeine Zeitung* in 1966. Nolte discussed the "final solution of the Jewish question" as a defensive response by Hitler to the mass murder the German Leader believed that the Bolsheviks and their Jewish allies would possibly visit upon the Germans. Historically, the Bolsheviks had killed untold numbers of the Russian upper and middle classes, and those suspected of anti-Semitism. They had starved to death millions of small farmers or "kulaks" in Ukraine, and massacred tens of thousands of the Polish upper classes at Katyn and elsewhere, that the advancing Germans had exhumed.

Elsewhere Mr. Nolte added the thought that Hitler might have felt justified in his violent measures against the Jewish population of Europe after "Chaim Weizmann's statement, in the first days of September 1939, that in this war the Jews of all the world would fight on England's side." "It unleashed a political storm in Germany and abroad." (The New York Times Book Review. Berghan, V. reviewed *Forever in the Shadow of Hitler* Translated by J. Knowlton and T. Cates. Humanities Press, and *The Path to Genocide*, Browning, C. Cambridge.)

There are said to be about 500 Holocaust hate-Nazi films, a continuing genre, while the Nazis made only three anti-Jewish films out of some 1,200, before and after they controlled film making in Germany. What are the possible motivations for this phenomenal continuous reprojection of an historical event?

The stock answer for the films, museums, compulsory curricula on the holocaust, etc. is to demonstrate the evil results of Intolerance. The Jewish nationalist agenda is apparently to insure that *Never Again* will anti-Semitism be tolerated or unpunished. A philosemitic climate of opinion "Holostatically," or "Holocaustically" controlled, has been created over the Western world. Anti-Semitism to Jewish imperialists is any criticism of Jews or their acts, implied or direct. That is why Jewish dissenters and dissidents are sometimes denounced as anti-Semitic or even anti-Jewish, by the Jewish Establishment. Philosemitism, with immunity from criticism, produces a culture distortion in the development of the Western tradition. As the late Alan Bloom said once on television, there has been no "Right" in western political life since the Second World War, only a dull substitute conservatism.

Separate church and state, mosque and state, synagogue and state? Some can, increasing numbers cannot. For many Jews in the United States, "the state" of greatest concern has been the state of Israel, that they have done so much to create and sustain.

"There is no more emotional, controversial, enigmatic, or dramatic political and strategic alliance in the history of the United States than its relation with the State of Israel. Americans look at Israel in the 1990s and wonder: Why does America send billions of dollars every year to a tiny country on the eastern edge of the Mediterranean?" Was this written by rightist-extremists, neo-this and that? It is on the cover jacket of *Friends in Deed: Inside the U.S.-Israeli Alliance* by two Israeli experts (New York: Hyperion, 1994). Words like these can end the career of a politician. After complaining in the Senate, "Here we are voting another $50 million for schools and hospitals in Israel, while I can't get $7 million for roads in Arkansas," chairman of the Senate Foreign Relations Committee for many years, J. William Fulbright said on the CBS program Face the Nation, 15 April 1973:

> The United States is subservient to Israel. Israel controls the Senate. The great majority of the Senate of the United States, somewhere around 80 percent, are completely in support of Israel, anything Israel wants. This has been demonstrated time and again, and this has made it difficult for the [U.S.] government.

Was this AS? Or was defeating Fulbright because of it anti-American? Pro-Israel fund raisers lined up for his opponent, and he was defeated.

Was this just "history" and are circumstances now different in Washington? The 2 September 1994 issue of *Ma'Ariv*, a prominent Israeli daily, had an article "The Jews who run Clinton's court." It quotes the rabbi of the Adath Yisrael synagogue in Washington, D.C. as saying "for the first time in American history…the U.S. has no longer a government of Goyim [Gentiles], but an administration in which the Jews are full partners in the decision making at all levels." Is this AS to denounce or believe?

What most non-Jews do not know is that there are probably half-a-million Jews, observant and reform, who oppose the state of Israel. Many observant Jews believe that the Israeli state is an abomination that can only delay the redemption of the Jewish people. "The Satmars have blamed the Nazi Holocaust on the Zionists, saying it was God's punishment for their efforts to establish a Jewish state prematurely, before the coming of the Messiah" (*The International Herald Tribune* 8 Je. 1994). They stated their beliefs to all authorities, beginning when the British first had the League of Nations Mandate for Palestine. They eschew El Al and all that! Other Jews have reconciled their Judaism, which they saw strictly as a religion, and the styles of Western thought.

In Russia, where Jews like Lazar Kaganovich and Lavrenti P. Beria, held top positions for much of the time of the Bolshevik and Stalinist dictatorship, Zionist activism and propaganda after the founding of the state of Israel, with pressure for Jewish emigration, separated many Jews as alien with a foreign agenda.

The fact that President Kennedy wrote a "Dear Alfred" letter to Lillienthal on 30 Sept. 1960, saying "I wholly agree with you that American partisanship in the Arab-Israeli conflict is dangerous to both the U.S. and the free world," supports speculation that Kennedy's assassination was masterminded by Israel's Mossad or secret service agents. The Mossad are super-specialists in political assassination and cover-up. Another example of such activity has been exposed by Robert C. McFarlane, President Ronald Reagan's National Security Adviser. On 3 July 1985, he was visited by David Kimche, officially director of Israel's Foreign Ministry, but behind the facade a top Mossad agent. At a secret White House meeting, the Israeli envoy proposed a plan to assassinate Iran's leader, the Ayatollah Ruholla Khomeini, if the United States government "supported" the operation. This was the opening move in what has become known as the Iran-Contra scandal. (McFarlane, R. *Special Trust.* NY: Cadell & Davies, 1994)

I have met a Palestinian who, as a child in a refugee camp experienced Israeli bombing – American planes, American napalm. He has vivid recall of the children with flesh burning, that could not be extinguished, neither could their screams. Abie Nathan, who for twenty years broadcast *The Voice of Peace*, from a freighter "somewhere in the Mediterranean," explained his motivation. "I feel I've done a lot of killing as a pilot in the air force," he said. "I've seen the victims that I've killed. I helped drive Arabs from their homes. I've seen misery all over the world. Today, for the first time, there is some light" (*Manhattan Jewish Sentinel*. 16 Fe. 1994, 3A).

Nathan was referring to the very limited peace agreement that enabled Yasir Arafat of the Palestinian Liberation Organization, on 2 July 1994 to pass the Jabaliya refugee camp, the place that marked the outbreak of the Childrens Uprising, that they called the *Intifada*, in 1987.

At a demonstration at the funeral of a Palestinian teenager killed by Israeli soldiers, two children were shot, including an 11-year old girl. The bullet was of a low-caliber kind fired by Israeli Army snipers who were supposed to aim at ringleaders of demonstrations. Mr. Bernard Mills, the British director in Gaza of the United Nations Relief and Works Agency, said angrily: "If the ringleader was 11, she must have had a gang of six-year-olds." History has nothing to compare with the Childrens Uprising but the Childrens Crusade of the Middle Ages. We have witnessed a seven-year revolt by children against a modern army of occupation.

Even according to the *New York Times*, "more than 1,000" were shot or beaten to death over the six and a half years of the Childrens Uprising [*NYT* 2 Jy. 1994, 8:2]. Thousands more were clubbed on the head and body, many brain-damaged and or their limbs deliberately broken.

Judith Viorst, Jewish author of books for children and some for adults, joined a party of 14 men and women who traveled to Israel, Gaza, and the West Bank in June 1988, in search of better understanding of the region. Writing of her experiences, she significantly started with an account of their visit to Yad Vashem, Israel's memorial to "the Holocaust dead," and ends with a passage which begins, "At Yad Vashem, the Holocaust images speak about survival and humanity…"

The article includes the following experience:

At a hospital in Gaza, I visited four young boys—skinny dark-haired kids a lot like mine. Except they had decided to bust out of their dead-end lives and had wound up badly beaten by Israeli soldiers. One boy speaking English, told us his arms had been broken twice—broken, set in a cast, broken again. And then he added three words that brought tears to my eyes and actually made me gasp with shock: They're not human.

This isn't the kind of statement I ever expected to hear about a Jew (*NYT* 9 Jy. 1988, Op-Ed page).

The response of then Israeli Defense Minister, Yitzhak Rabin, was to try and tranquilize European and American critics of his policies with a guilt injection: "Let them first search their own deeds in the recent and distant past before they dare besmirch the character of the State of Israel and the I.D.F. soldiers," he said in Jerusalem on 1 March 1988, using the initials of the Israeli Defense Force. "I am the government in the territories..." he announced with the grandiosity that is the complement of paranoia, on 21 June 1988.

Reporting in the *New York Times* the next day, correspondent Joel Brinkley wrote, "By all accounts," Rabin's policies provided what most Israelis want. "Israelis overwhelmingly favor what some polls refer to as heavy-handed force against violent Palestinians. That attitude, said a senior aide to Foreign Minister Shimon Peres, is a reflection of Israelis' 'basic frustration, humiliation and hatred of the Arabs.'"

"Mr. Rabin is the architect of Israel's 'force, might, beatings' policy in the occupied territories." Of course, there is more to one of the most oppressive foreign occupations in the modern era, than would fill all the Holocaust museums. Thousands of Palestinians in refugee camps – but thousands in Israeli *concentration camps*. Amnesty International reports of *The Methods of Torture*, confirmed by former members of Mossad and Shin Beth in their memoirs, give details of its institutionalization of brutality and torture in treatment of Palestinians. There are reports of gross violations of human rights to the U.N. Special Committee on Human Rights in the Occupied Territories, and other accounts that are sampled in *Behind the Balfour Declaration* (John, R. 1988, 11-15).

Here are some excerpts from old reports which were hardly noticed in the world press, and soon forgotten by most of us. The mass of similar material is huge.

On 5 December 1968 the International Red Cross reported:

On a visit which was carried out without the presence of an observer, 81 prisoners were found huddled in one cell. The prisoners all declared that they were not allowed to leave their cells, even to use the toilets or washing facilities. They had to use the cell tap which was situated only 15 centimeters from the level of the floor.

In 1990 Victor Ostrovsky, a former Mossad agent, became internationally known when the state of Israel attempted to ban his first account of Mossad cruelty to Palestinians and other misdeeds. His book *By Way of Deception* was followed four years later by *The Other Side of Deception*, that further revealed secrets from one man's experience of the Dark Side.

The point of re-recording even this very small sample of infamy, is to offer even a taste of the blood and anguish that has flowed from the bodies of Palestinians - from the inextinguishable fire of the flesh from American napalm, from bombs, guns, knives, clubs, and instruments of torture used by the Israelis. Can it be an antidote to the brainwashing with five hundred hate films and the Niagara of the Holocaust? Great men from an earlier freer era before tales of the "holocaust" established a Western guilt syndrome, men like Arnold Toynbee, and the philosopher Bertrand Russell, whom I met after his eightieth birthday, spoke out against Jewish injustice, so obvious to those who care, but so seldom noticed or remembered by the American and European public.

On 2 February 1970, the day before he died, Bertrand Russell addressed a message to an International Conference of Parliamentarians on the Middle East Crisis, in which he called for vigorous condemnation of Israeli aggression "throughout the world."

For over 20 years Israel has expanded by force of arms. After every stage in this expansion Israel has appealed to "reason" and has suggested "negotiations." This is the traditional role of the imperial power, because it wishes to consolidate with the least difficulty what it has taken already by violence. Every new conquest becomes the new basis of the proposed negotiations from strength which ignores the injustice of the previous aggression. The aggression committed by Israel must be condemned not only because no state has the right to annex foreign territory, but because every expansion is also an experiment to discover how much more aggression the world will tolerate.

We are frequently told that we must sympathize with Israel because of the suffering of the Jews in Europe at the hands of the Nazis. I see in this suggestion no reason to perpetuate any suffering. What Israel is doing today cannot be condoned, and to invoke the horrors of the past, to justify those of the present, is gross hypocrisy.

Arnold Toynbee, who probably drafted the secret document on British commitments to King Husein, Sherif of Mecca, for the inner group at the Versailles Peace Conference, went on to become one of the century's outstanding world historians. He wrote in Volume VIII of his great *A Study of History*:

> The Jews' immediate reaction to their own experience was to become persecutors in their turn for the first time since A.D. 135, and this at the first opportunity that had arisen for them to inflict on other human beings who had done the Jews no injury, but who happened to be weaker than they were, some of the wrongs and sufferings that had been inflicted on the Jews.
>
> In A.D. 1949, the Jews knew from personal experience what they were doing, and it was their supreme tragedy that the lesson learned by them from their encounter with the Nazi Gentiles should have been not to eschew but to imitate some of their evil deeds that the Nazis had committed against the Jews (289-290).

This judgment made him the target for attacks familiar to anyone who has dared to tell the truth on these issues. The attacks were *ad hominem* rather than relevant to his subject matter. In 1960 he wrote in Volume XII:

> The seizure of the houses, lands, and property of the 900,000 Palestinian Arabs who are now refugees is on a moral level with the worst crimes and injustices committed, during the last four or five centuries, by Gentile Western European conquerors and colonists overseas. This is still my judgment on the Zionist movement's record in Palestine since it began to resort to violence there (627).

The Jesuit theologian, and former professor at the Vatican's Pontifical Biblical Institute, author of *The Keys of This Blood, The Final Conclave* and other extraordinary works, told us he had worked with the influential Jesuit cardinal Augustin Bea and Pope John XXIII on the Second Vatican Council from 1958 to 1964 (the First was in 1870). When we met him the next time, he said that a main activity of his on the Councils had been working with the international Jewish leaders who had come to Rome to have critical references to Jews removed from all Roman Catholic source materials. After reading *The Palestine Diary* (John, R. 1970) a diplomatic history of British, American and United Nations intervention in Palestine from 1914 to 1948, he said that what he now knew about the Zionist Jews and Palestine and the Palestinians, made him now regret much of what he had accomplished.

The great teacher of Mythology, Joseph Campbell, whom I first met at the Cooper Union in New York years before, at the Open Eye on 3 March 1981, cited support for the state of Israel as an example of the power of ancient myth: "To have a modern 20th century political situation with the United States standing for Israel because God gave that to them is hard to believe – this is sheer mythology, and we're in it up to our necks!." Campbell believed Judaism to be the most materialistic of common religions. We did not meet Mahatma Gandhi, but he believed, "The real Jerusalem is the spiritual Jerusalem. Thus the Jews can realize this in any part of the world."

In fact, the Jewish account in the bank of public sympathy has been long overdrawn, firstly paid out in money – $150,000,000,000 from the United States and Germany, and paid out in suffering inflicted upon a conquered people – Palestinians.

There is a Latin expression of Seneca's, made to Lucilius, *Demere rebus tumultum*, that translates: *One must separate things from the noise they are making.* Separate the Holocaust from Israel and Palestine. Because the hullabaloo of the Holocaust almost drowned out the cries of suffering of the Palestinians.

The never-ending stream of advertising messages on the Holocaust are put out to give the impression that political Jews still have credit to cash in, and to give the impression that we are guilty and owe them more. They are bankrupt. They have lived long on international welfare. Cut it off and they will be the better for that. Like street beggars, they have rattled the cup for donations and sympathy, claiming disability from old injuries, and immunity from criticism. But in the name of Israel the worst of crimes have committed: a sufferer gaining power over others making the oppressed suffer. Jews were called *Untermenschen*: Palestinians are called cockroaches.

But there are righteous Jews. My friend for many years, and former State Dept. official Alfred M. Lilienthal, wrote on his 80th birthday: "My Jewish brethren are caught in the unbreakable vise of nationalism-tribalism which blinds them from seeing that the worship of the Israeli state is gradually supplanting the worship of Yahweh."

Finally, can one go one better in this issue than citing Chaim Weizmann, the leading engineer and first president of Israel? Who wrote:

"I am certain that the world will judge the Jewish State by what it will do to the Arabs" (*Trial and Error*. New York: Harper, 1949, 462).

Nearly a half-century later, **the world can judge** *by what has been done* **to the Arabs.**

I look at today's *Wall Street Journal*: "An Israeli interrogator was suspended after pathologists said a Palestinian prisoner was tortured to death last week, security sources said. Separately, Prime Minister Rabim told his cabinet that he personally had approved plans to confiscate Arab-owned land in Jerusalem to make way for construction of two Jewish neighborhoods." **1st. May 1995**, 1:3)

For years the several thousand foreigners making official visits to Israel each year submitted to the ritual of being taken to Yad Vashem, the memorial in Jerusalem to the Jews who died in World War II. How many Christian visitors have passed by Palestinians who fell among thieves, clicking their cameras where the Israeli guide directed – at whitened sepulchers?

However, stepping back from the day's news, from criticism of merciless political Judaism, from Philosemitism, gives the possibility of the evolutionary perspective. In summary, Jewish tactics are expressions of an evolutionary strategy for survival. Religion, prescriptions for economic and social interactions within the group and with those outside it, coordinate towards this end. "Is it good for the Jews?" has been a historically successful criterion, a biologically and ethologically based question promoting survival. This insight provides a basis for evaluation of Jewish expression in word and act. Host populations' reactions to the strategy answer the ADL's question to Dr. Glock.

Chairman of the Jewish Agency, Avraham Burg: "If real peace comes to Israel, the question will be asked: Can we, and how do we survive without an external enemy?" (Jerusalem 23 F. 1995)

5

The Equalist Dogma

The evolution of "Western Christianity" and Euro-American culture into a rational system of ideas and ethics based upon an integration of what we know at the end of the twentieth century has been aborted. It has been suppressed. Suppression is maintained by an invisible force-field of which one is hardly aware unless one comes up against it. But there is increasing complaint that public discourse on certain issues is suppressed because of being politically "incorrect." State Communism may be nearly gone, but Marxist, equalist and religious dogmas and distortions remain and are the bases for social action. The application of these dogmas – since they are false, has given results different from those advertised, and perhaps intended, to obtain public support or acquiescence. This is why Western civilization is in decline, in retreat, and why only religious fundamentalisms are able to attract new recruits for their forces in the field of belief and action, for they rely on faith not fact.

Increasingly in the last half of the twentieth century, legislators and politically appointed socially activist judges in the United States, led the Western world in restricting the freedom of people to unite their common affections in societies and to speak their minds. Children have been bused out of neighborhoods where they lived, householders have been compelled by judges to subsidize housing for people who are not part of their community. Employers and admissions officers have been plagued by ethnic quotas and guidelines they must fulfill, and legal sanctions and monetary punishments if they do not.[*] Educators are burdened with the issues resulting from obligatory ethnic diversity of students. Should education be in each of the ethnic histories and cultures – diversity, or is it still permissible to teach Western history and tradition?

There are struggles in the teaching of the Western Tradition in schools and colleges. The addition of comparative studies is appropriate when our tradition has been integrated by our children into their personae. Children of African and other non-Western

---

[*]An African American and his supervisor were awarded $89 million in damages in 1994 for wrongful dismissal. The company maintained that their work was unsatisfactory.

53

origins should have their own tradition priority, unless they choose otherwise. As Adam Clayton Powell said inspirationally to African-American students at U.C.L.A. years ago, "Black is not just a color – it's an experience – it's a history."

Social services are specially devised to help immigrants from non-Western cultures, and paid for by taxes on indigenous workers. Election ballots may be in foreign languages – Spanish in the U.S.A. and as many as five in parts of Great Britain, for example.

These conflicts and confusions are results of Egalitarian Theology or the Equalist Dogma. The dogmatists and "true believers" increasingly controlled our media, our institutions and foundations, in the last half of the twentieth century. It has been expressed in legislation, court decisions, media bias, witch-hunting and harassment of dissidents. Many Christians, Humanists, Jews, Moonies, Moslems, Ba'hai's and so on are adherents of Equalism as part of their faith-belief. Theory and knowledge have been suppressed and removed from influence upon policy.

Historically, truly Liberal reformers, such as Margaret Sanger in the United States, had some success in the early twentieth century. Marxism attempted integration of theory and policy. It failed because its dogma barred facts of life. An extreme example was the acceptance of the teaching of Lysenko in the U.S.S.R., that manipulation of the environment of seeds would change the inherited characteristics of plants. But the Marxist infatuation with environmentalism paralleled western establishment censure of data on heredity and eugenics.

In the century's later half, major policies of western societies such as poverty programs have also failed for the same reason. They have been based on the equalist dogma, shared with Marxism. From mid-century, the American evolutionary Qualist philosopher Charles Smith, taught that Equalism was the dominant world religion promoted by the establishments of the then two superpowers, the U.S.A. and the U.S.S.R. "Most freethinkers, rationalists, secularists, atheists, and humanists have joined Christians and Communists in the war on mechanical materialism applied to man and society. All these schools of associaters are united in the struggle to prevent reasoning, causal thinking, concerning man; to prevent judging by samples, valuing intrinsic qualities, and considering social and racial results" (Smith, Charles. 1956. *Sensism: The Philosophy of the West*. New York: The Truth

Seeker Co. vol. 2, p.1573). Smith defined **qualism**: valuing intrinsic qualities; **equalist**: one who values extrinsic qualities, which are the same for all members of the class, rather than intrinsic, which vary with individuals and with varieties within the class. **Qualities**. There are three kinds of qualities: *primary*, such as size, shapes and motion; *secondary*, such as a name an essence and a value. A tertiary quality is not a part of that of which it is a quality. Primary and secondary qualities are intrinsic; tertiary qualities are extrinsic. (Ibid. Glossary.)

The Equalist ideology has been expressed in many ways. In the 1960s as "the Generation Gap." We heard Margaret Mead tell a group of largely young intellectuals at a meeting of the American Academy for the Advancement of Science that "there is nothing that your parents' generation can teach you which is of any use to you," that is, they had no special knowledge worth imparting.

There was the unisex movement, that taught the differences between human males and females were superficial or environmental. A corollary was that a family consisting of male and female parents was superfluous and "single" parenthood could be an ideal; for children may be raised just as well by a single male or female, and differing male and female role models were part of an obsolete oppressive system.

Heredity of humans was inconsequential, like differences in female and male thought and behavior, environment eclipsed all other factors. A major expression was the dogma that differences between races were superficial and inconsequential also. The Constitution was a consensual expression of their world-view in the political language and self-image of its Framers and of their people. Earl Warren and his comrades on the Supreme Court inserted revolutionary meanings into the words and concepts of the U.S. Constitution without altering a single letter of its revered textual form. What had been constitutional for one hundred and seventy years became unconstitutional, and had to be abandoned, in Felix Frankfurter's phrase, "with all deliberate speed."

The late Senate Republican leader, Everett Dirksen, told me how he had come to vote for the 1964 Civil Rights Act. He said he had disagreed with it saying, "I do not believe a chromatic scale should decide which school a child should attend." Dirksen said that there had been an impartial survey to pick the location of the Fermi nuclear particle accelerator. His home state of Illinois had been chosen. He was told that if he did not vote for the Act, the project would be located elsewhere, a loss of a billion dollars to his state. He called this "arm twisting." Is it representative government? Is it democracy? ("Arm twisting" was used by the Clinton administration to push the North American Free Trade Agreement through Congress.)

Eureka – I have found [it] – is the motto of the State of California. It is attributed to Archimedes on his discovery of a method of determining the ratio of weight to volume. Eureka brings feelings of elation and optimism. Such a feeling of optimism came with the Enlightenment. By the time of the American Revolution, it was being expressed as a future of life, liberty, and the pursuit of happiness, or *la chasse au bonheur*, as they said in France. But the joy of Eureka is not necessarily associated with discovery of scientific truth. The early Christians experienced the sense of great joy and inward freedom from the turmoil of their world derived from their possession of the Good News, the Glad Tidings of the Gospel. (In these times of Western cultural, social, political turmoil, "born-again" Christians, and Moslem fundamentalist converts, and other dependents on faith may feel the same.) But just as with time and change, the Christian grandiose sense of possible union with the resurrected Lord of the Universe became overlaid with feeling a fear of damnation and estrangement, with Western Christendom first burning people as heretics on 28 December 1022 in Orleans, so in a lesser way, Western society – following the United States, is now overlaid with fear of expressing certain ideas that are heretical and fear of loosing control of its "mixed multitudes," a fear of dissolution. Again, with so much more information, we need a new enlightenment and dedication to free inquiry. "There is an urgent and critical need to bring the laws of the life sciences for which there is good evidence into courts, congresses, and parliaments, and into the consciousness of our peoples" (John, R. Improving Human Consciousness, in *Applied Systems and Cybernetics* [ed. G.E. Lasker], Pergamon, 1981, Vol. 1, 131-135).

The Roman Catholic Bishops of the United States at the Ecumenical Council in Rome in 1963 pressed for the adoption of a document stating that qualitative differences between races is contrary to the church's fundamental beliefs. Its adoption was followed by the leaders of other denominations adopting similar resolutions.

In 1964 when issues like "affirmative action," or quotas favoring "minorities" were being debated in the United States Congress, Dwight. J. Ingle of the University of Chicago reminded the scientific community that "the equality of man is social, legal, and ethical rather than a biological concept, for among living things nothing is equal to or identical with anything else" (Ingle, D.J. Science , 146, 375-9). In 1969 the National Academy of Sciences declined to study the hereditary aspects of human quality; Academy President Frederick Seitz saying that "the conduct of such research at the present would tend to heighten current social tensions to a very destructive degree."

"It used to be taken for granted that it was not only ethically right for scientists to make public their discoveries, it was their duty to do so. Secrecy, the withholding of information, and the refusal to communicate knowledge were rightly regarded as cardinal sins against the scientific ethos. This is true no more," wrote Hans Eysenck, professor of psychology at London University's Institute of Psychiatry in 1975. (British Assn. for the Advancement of Science, New Issue. No. 1.)

Only in the last chapter of *Sociobiology*, published in 1975, did E.O. Wilson write of humans, raising challenging questions and possibilities for human relevance of his findings and speculations. He argued that warfare, dislike of foreigners or xenophobia, the relative dominance of males, and occasional individual altruism, were all patterns of behavior springing in part from our primordial compulsion to protect and propagate our genes. Unaware that he had crossed the invisible boundary set up by the establishment thought-police, Wilson says, "I stumbled into a mine field." The agents of thought "correctness" nearest him at Harvard University were the Marxist biologists Richard Lewontin and Leon Kamin, and their associate Stephen J. Gould, – important names, intelligent, brilliantly argumentative people, brought up in the Reformed or Humanist Jewish tradition, – attacked Wilson for promoting an updated version of social Darwinism and providing justification for racism (an appellation first used as *racisme* by Leon Trotsky circa 1922), sexism, and nationalistic aggression.

His opponents may have thought Wilson "washed-up" after a scientific conference in 1975, when a radical activist dumped a pitcher of water on Wilson's head while shouting, "You're all wet!" To which Lewontin added academic ice by writing in the *Harvard Gazette* (16 Jan. 1976), "any investigations into the genetic control of human behavior is bound to produce a pseudo-science that will inevitably be misused." But Wilson not only went back to his ants, but to observation and theorizing. In 1981 he published *Genes, Mind, and Culture*, that Lewontin falsely declared in *The Sciences* (July/August) "contains no information about genes, mind, or culture – and certainly nothing about their interconnections." In 1992 Wilson published *The Diversity of Life*. It became a best-seller and Wilson became widely known and admired for his brilliance, almost impossible to denounce with the contemporary equivalents of witchcraft: racism, sexism, anti-Semitism, homophobia, elitism, neo-isolationism, and neo-Nazism.... The utilization of socio-biological precepts, which are in the line of succession of the Western tradition, would allow the development of a more rational political system; one that encourages "the maximum personal growth" of humans while preserving the environment. Wilson believes that human sociobiology has the potential to "subsume most of the social sciences and a great deal of philosophy," and bring about profound changes in philosophy and religion (*Scientific American*, April 1994 p.36).

At the 1977 meeting of the British Association for the Advancement of Science, Sir Andrew Huxley spoke on the need for the findings of scientific research to be independent of wishes and fears about their possible applications, a distinction between fact and value. He drew a comparison between the violence of the nineteenth century debate occasioned by the *Origin of Species*, in which his grandfather had played so prominent a part, and the contemporary one on racial difference. He defined racism as the subjugation of one race by another (Huxley, A. *The Times Higher Educ. Supp.*, 2 Sept. 1977.). The speech was criticized in an unprecedented, because unscientific, editorial in *Nature*, which had recently come under the control of a multinational corporation. The editor charged Huxley to explain "why we are better off with the knowledge than without it" (Editorial. *Nature*. 29 Sept. 1977, 366).

While books that supported the faith of Equalism had the full support of virtually all media in Europe and America – like Ashley Montague's *Mans Most Dangerous Myth* that went into over thirty editions, scientists with contrary data found the gates of scientific exposition shut against them. The suppression of research and repression and victimization of researchers in these areas in recent times was reviewed by Roger Pearson in *Race, Intelligence and*

Bias in Academe (Scott-Townsend, a small independent publisher, 1991).

The transparent surface of suppression was broken by publication of *The Bell Curve* in 1994. Writing in the British *Spectator* (26 N. 1994, 31) Paul Johnson reminded that "There was a time when Americans led the world in saying what they thought. That is how they are portrayed by Dickens, Trollope and Thackeray ...Now educated Americans, especially the ruling class of businessmen, politicians, academics and media people, are terrified of opening their mouths on any topic even vaguely connected with race...I believe, however, that a change may be coming. The publication of Charles Murray and Richard Herrnstein's *The Bell Curve* marks a turning point in the race debate....[But] Attacks on Murray have been highly personal, mendacious and directed to making him unemployable." (See also Editorial. *Intelligence* 19, 263-280, 1994) This is "the power of the purse" that presumably governs relevant editorials in *Nature*, which in 1992 likened the possibility of finding significant group differences in brain size to contradicting accepted views of an ellipsoid earth, continental drift, and relativity theory (Maddox. J. 358, 187).

The shuttered facade of freedom of inquiry and discussion that exists in Western countries, behind which is suppression of criticism of issues vital to the future of their peoples was temporarily illuminated in Britain by publication of *The Bell Curve*. A courageous reviewer was able to open a window briefly with a review of the book. She titled it, "The Truth That Dares Not Whisper Its Name." The writer, Lynnette Burrows, wrote an objective review, and then from her window condemned the efforts of equalists to suppress discussion of the issues raised in the book. Most of Europe, she said, "...Has embarked upon a love affair with multi-racialism that has been at best undemocratic and at worst like colonialism in reverse. Country after country has been settled by millions of foreigners without the acquiescence of the indigenous population."

And further, "What is sinister...is the fact that we are not even allowed to discuss the continued settlement of our country by upwards of 50,000 Asians a year, despite the growing signs that they feel their numbers now constitute a nation within a nation" (*Sunday Telegraph*. 16 O. 1994).

The editor of the American magazine *The New Republic*, Andrew Sullivan writing in *The Sunday Times News Review* (23 O.

1994), described the confrontation in his office on whether to print an essay by Murray and Herrnstein: "Tempers flared, insults were hurled, for a while some people would hardly speak to me. One editor sent me a letter accusing me of committing an act of 'moral and intellectual evil.' Another yelled in my office: 'But these guys are Nazis!'…It soon became apparent that I was not dealing with an issue in which rational debate was going to hold sway…."

This is the Orwellian state of discourse in the press and other media of which "the people" are unaware, because few uncontrolled messages reach them. "When the press accuses, the accusation is bigger news than the reply. Charges, indictments and convictions are given more space and bigger type than acquittals, vindications and retractions" (Clurman, R. 1988. *Beyond Malice.*). Then there is the critical matter of selection of matter that the media may use. Many books and frequent quotes in the media reported fraud by Sir Cyril Burt in his use of data on the importance of heredity. Burt was portrayed in popular print and television docudrama as a cold, ruthless and dishonest crank. When "evidence" against him was refuted, that received no coverage.

It has been theorized that what distinguishes influential egalitarians from other cultural elites is their rejection of authority and their preference for equality of results over equality of opportunity. "Thus egalitarians may be expected to prefer reduction of differences – between races, or income levels, or sexes, or parents and children, teachers and students, authorities and citizens" (Wildavsky, A. 1991. *The Rise of Radical Egalitarianism.*).

Webster's *Third International* sums up egalitarianism as "the suppression of all distinctions between individuals and groups as inherently unjust: an extreme political and social leveling."

In early 1995, the president of Rutgers University in New Jersey blamed "three words jumbled together" in a talk with faculty members for creating the false impression that he believed a "genetic hereditary background" made it hard for African-American students to do well on college entrance examinations. "Let me unequivocally make it clear that the view that genetic and hereditary factors determine ability and achievement is dead wrong," he said. "The idea is precisely opposed to my beliefs. I regret it, I do regret it, I certainly regret these comments." Previously at Tulane University, where he helped increase the

African-American student population from 1 to 10 percent, at Rutgers, Francis Lawrence raised millions of dollars for scholarships and programs benefiting only them and Hispanic students. He presided over the opening of a $1 million cultural center for African-Americans, and was instrumental in the passage of an "anti-hate speech" code on the university's three major campuses. But a life of good works was hardly a defense against damnation.

Apart from the specific argument, these few words and the storm on campus and extensive press and broadcast coverage that followed them, demonstrate that there are contemporary heresies; that free inquiry and free expression of views are suppressed. *Mea culpa, mea culpa* . . . What university president Francis L. Lawrence had said was: "The average S.A.T.'s for African-Americans is 750. Do we set standards in the future so we don't admit anybody? Or do we deal with a disadvantaged population that doesn't have that genetic, hereditary background to have a higher average?"

He had crossed the line of the politically correct by stating that genetics and heredity are major factors in performance. To understand the fierce reaction of "many young black students, whose anger is directed not only at the president, but also at the world beyond their dorms and classrooms" (*NYT.* 10 F. 1995, B5:5), we must consider the messages they receive from that world. (See our chapter Mens Sana)

In early 1995 also, there was vigorous opposition to President Clinton's nomination of Dr. Henry W. Foster for Surgeon General of the U.S.A. He had an unusual record of work to reduce teenage pregnancy and promote responsible parenthood. But he was attacked by the Religious Right for having performed legal abortions, and from Left and Right for having performed hysterectomies on severely retarded women. A professor of obstetrics and gynecology at the University of Pennsylvania testified that "it was not just a matter to provide pregnancy protection, but also hygiene." He added, "In the course of menstruation, they would not be able to care for themselves and would have to be restrained in order to put a tampon in, if you could get one in." This is an attack upon rational behavior. It shows the regression that has taken place since the United States was a leader in eugenics policies in the first half of the century. A hereditary form of mental deficiency or idiocy is a documented fact. But the contrary is suggested in popular media.

Earlier in our own century there were European and American thinkers whose ideas were sometimes called Naturalism, who attempted to bring what they understood were the laws of nature into public decisions. Margaret Sanger, the pioneer for family planning and the liberation of women from involuntary pregnancy, believed in "more children from the fit, less from the unfit - that is the chief issue of birth control." Charles Darwin's cousin, the "Victorian genius" Francis Galton, who died in 1911, had truly liberal followers of the hopeful idea that utilizing principles of heredity could reduce disease, criminality, idiocy, and the proportion of those unable to care for themselves, making our world a happier place. The United States was a leader in eugenic legislation at the beginning of this century. Contemporary education and media are dismissive of Supreme Court Justice Holmes' decision in the case of three generations of imbeciles who had a familial, hereditary mental retardation, who were reproducing frequently and could not support themselves. In affirming a lower court decision for the compulsory sterilization of members of that family, he said, "Three generations of imbeciles is enough." We have moved very far away from that. (Buck v. Bell. 274 U.S. 200 1927. "An Act of Virginia…recites that the health of the patient and the welfare of society may be promoted by the sterilization of mental defectives, under careful safeguard, etc.…")

Globalism and Equalism

For the last fifty years Caucasoid societies have been living with an entirely different system of values. On one hand, Marxism and international socialism declare all workers to be equal, no matter what your race, ethnic background, religion, sex, or disability. On the other hand, for international capitalism we are all consumers. We have the "United Colors of Benetton" advertising theme, in which you see people of different races all wearing the same types of clothing. That is a marketing victory. If promoters can get the tribal people we want to save in the rain forests of the Amazon to wear Benetton, if someone can get them to wear sanitary napkins, or shoes, that would be a tremendous marketing victory. The promoter's reward in the empire of commerce could be the coveted title C.E.O. and the order of the golden parachute!

The Benetton advertising is also a political statement. Luciano Bennetton has some 7,000 stores around the world. In 1992 he had his picture taken with Fidel Castro, whom he invited to become a "teacher of revolution" at a new design school near Treviso, Italy; demonstrating Bennetton's philosophy that political discourse or propaganda for social change can serve product advertising. "A favorite theme is equality, with attempts to blur the racial and cultural distinctions that would separate people." "We tend to be way out there," said their director of communications for North America. *"But advertising of this kind had power to change a value system"* (*N.Y.T.* 29 Jy. 93). Bennetton is observant of the equalist religion but distinguishes his advertising by putting equalism "up-front" with shocking emphasis. The messages of other Western media are similarly subversive, but usually more subtle.

The paradigm for that type of thinking is this expression which so many people have taken to themselves, the "global village," a wonderful metaphor of potted ideas. In the global village there are no color, racial or ethnic differences, no hereditary differences in intelligence or anything like that, we are all consumers. Just as a few years ago, we were told that male and female were largely social conventions, differences superficial, *Unisex* was conceived as a new word and marketing concept! Now there is so much evidence from the womb on that there really is a difference, that the position is untenable, but some unisex stores still remain to remind us of that construct. We do not realize that the egalitarian dogma is part of a movement which has been engineered for us. In a book published in 1991, an official of the Council on Foreign Relations tells us that the General Agreement on Tariffs and Trade of 1957 had "the goal of building a unified and integrated global system" (Aho, C.M. 1991. *The Growth of Regional Trading Blocs in the Global Economy*, eds. R.S. Belous and S.S. Hartley, National Planning Association, Washington, D.C. Aho is director of economic studies at the Council on Foreign Relations.).

The important British historian with a Marxist perspective Eric Hobsbawm, contrasts the bureaucratic, conservative elements of the Communist system with the restless turbulence of international capitalism. Capitalism without a country destroys old familial solidarities and increases insecurity. The global economy, with transnational corporations, created a new international division of labor and the possibility of using offshore finance with no accountability. "The most convenient world for multinational giants is one populated by dwarf states or no states at all." Globalization deprives states of effective controls and "the interests of the various parts of the traditional social-democratic constituency" are diverging, and there have emerged new attempts by groups to separate and define their interests. Of this, he disapproves (Hobsbawm, E. *The Age of Extremes*. 1995). But Hobsbawm correctly "doublethinks" states (and sovereignty) as means for defense of the values of their peoples.

Both Communists, and global transnational capitalists and their corporations, could generally agree on central banking control, on the promotion of a common consumer market of blurred boundaries and one color. They would like one system of laws - which they would make, one armed force – which they would control. Globalism would impose, under a banner of global peace – global tyranny, a New World Order. The protagonists of these two systems have been the USSR and the USA.

In the USSR things did not work out very well economically for their people. A pre-Revolutionary large agricultural surplus for export was replaced by perennial scarcity, for example. In the USA, years of national decisions based upon spurious values have drawn upon the patrimony of generations, so that from being the world's biggest creditor, it is now the world's largest debtor, and the quality of life in its major cities has greatly deteriorated. So we must be very careful about wanting to follow either of these systems. These are two extremes.

We ought to be looking for the center. Just think what happens in American cities today. The statistics for murder in the capital city of the United States is ten murders a week. Every six minutes, a woman is raped in the United States - and those are only the ones we know about. Is there not something very wrong with that society too? Both these systems consider the most important differences between man and man to be economic. For both an international socialist and an international capitalist, if they bring thousands of non-Europeans into Germany or into France, or a hundred million more people into America, they just have to integrate more workers or more consumers. That is the way we are trained to think. That is the globalist, free market, or even communist way of looking at people, and not looking at them in terms of their identity, in terms of who they really are, in terms of how they think about themselves.

We should consider, as did the framers of the American Constitution and others, what we want for the next hundred years. What are the decisions about our habitats we must make? What makes America America? What makes France France? Is it because the people who live there have a special history? – They have special traditions, they have a language. People should have the opportunity to develop their cultures. Do we need more people to come here, even if the population declines, or do we need more housing, more roads, more concrete, more or bigger cities, more garbage...? Is that the future we want? Is not the enlightened solution for the developed countries to use systems analysis, to use cybernetics, for our needs? We should be giving back areas of territory, of land, to Nature, to the rest of what we are a part of, that we have taken. We have taken so much. We need to be giving some back to the rest of – to use the old fundamentalist word – Creation or rather – Evolution. In contemporary terms, to establish a new harmony between human and general ecology.

We need to make those decisions for ourselves now, and not allow this set pattern of thinking which we do not realize we have had imposed on us for the last half century, to dictate the decisions, but to use the disciplines and information we have. That is a wonderful opportunity.

For half a century The Sage of San Diego and his colleagues spoke out for free inquiry, and freedom to speak and publish on genetic and hereditary difference. For this, he was denounced and vilified during his lifetime by believers in the supernatural, by many atheists and humanists, as was Charles Smith, and after Johnson's death he was denounced in the very periodical that he edited for many years, and for the philosophic continuation of which he had provided the money in his last testament (*The Truth Seeker*).

We need to relate existing and new knowledge to understand and judge our value systems as they relate to biology and survival, and our quality of life for the next hundred years. We should be missionaries among our own peoples for the enhancement of the quality of life. We are for a human ecology which promotes it. We are for a new enlightenment based on what we know to support it.

Scientific integrity must still be defended and advocated. Philippe

Ruston of the University of Western Ontario suggests four principles for inquiry and the debate on these issues:

1. Seek the truth and speak it as you know it, directly and not in code.
2. Do not speculate about motives unless you have very good grounds for doing so. Integrity is the only character trait that is of concern when evaluating ideas and their impact.
3. Do not apologize for or act embarrassed about racially sensitive research or its results. To do so lends credence to the belief that you think you are doing something wrong.
4. Zealously protect freedom of scientific inquiry (*Intelligence.* 19, 275.).

Without comment, here is testimony on liberty of a man in public life for more than thirty years, Senator Bill Bradley, to the National Press Club, 9 Fe. 1995: "I decided I would no longer be restrained from saying what I really felt about issues, that there was a role in American politics for a truth teller and that I was going to try as much as possible to fill that role, because it was essential and because it actually fit my personality, and I had been kind of suppressing that part of my personality for a long time."

When such a bland member of the government admits that he has suppressed his views on "issues" for so long, it is appropriate to give weight to our charge that a great part of Western confusion is a result of suppression of facts and free discussion of issues to counter official disinformation. Yet, as in *1984*, Western peoples believe they live with liberty and democracy.

6

Mens Sana In Corpore Sano

The ovation swelled from the capacity audience which had braved 30-below wind chill in downtown St. Paul to witness a live broadcast of "A Prairie Home Companion." The native son understood that this rousing ovation could not possibly be for him. So he turned to greet African-American actor James Earl Jones, who had just walked out of the wings. "Minnesotans, bless their hearts, are an earnest people," Mr. Keillor said later. "They believe the harder they clap for James Earl Jones, the more it demonstrates they're not racists." The crowd granted him only polite applause, but Mr. Keillor was not surprised. "The only way I could get the kind of welcome James Earl Jones got here in Minnesota," he said a few days after the show, "was if I was suffering from a well-publicized fatal disease" (*NYT.* 27 Mr. 94 H 39).

In Brooklyn, New York, on 7 December 1993, Colin Ferguson loaded his 9-millimeter pistol, put 160 rounds of additional ammunition in his pockets, and took a train crowded with homebound commuters to Hicksville, Long Island. There he deliberately commenced firing on the packed passengers, killing five people and wounding 18 others. As he paused to reload, two brave men overpowered him.

Early in the morning of February 26, 1994 Dr. Baruch Goldstein loaded his automatic rifle and went to a mosque in Hebron in the West Bank area of the Jordan River, where the patriarch Abraham is said to be buried. Firing into the crowd kneeling at prayer, he emptied the magazine, killing 30 or more and wounding many others.

Ferguson, a Jamaican, deliberately set out to kill white people. Goldstein, a Jew who thought of himself as an Israeli, had gone to kill Palestinian Moslems.

Why? Is the fact that each had spent a significant part of their life in Brooklyn all they had in common?

67

As a child, Ferguson led a sheltered life in an affluent family in Jamaica, West Indies. He attended one the island's best schools. Its principal says he was a pleasant, punctual, well-behaved student who played cricket, was the star goalkeeper on the soccer team and graduated in the top third of his class. After graduation, his father got him a job, but died when Ferguson was 20. Looking to improve his prospects, he emigrated to the United States when he was 24. After a marriage that gave him citizenship and a temporary companion, and problems with jobs and college, in 1991 he moved to Brooklyn. A fall at one job gained him workers' compensation of $26,250 in September 1992.

From all accounts, Goldstein was a model student at the Yeshiva of Flatbush in Brooklyn, Yeshiva University and Einstein Medical School. He is said to have been a paradigm of self-sacrifice and devotion to others. "It is hard to believe that such a person could become a mass murderer solely as a result of the pressure of recent events...." notes liberal Rabbi Shlomo Sternberg (*NYT* 9 Mr. 1994. A14).

We have become accustomed to the concept of the "power of positive thinking," thanks in part to the precepts of people of every generation, at least from Dr. Coué to the late Norman Vincent Peale, or the latest "feel-good" book in paperback.

And the power of negative thinking?

Well, the positive proponents warn against it, some saying it can set you up for cancer, or shorten your life some other way through stress, depression.... In a major clinical study at Duke University, made public at a meeting of the Society of Behavioral Medicine on 15 April 1994, researchers reported that negative emotions, including feeling hostile, significantly reduced chances of survival from the effects of heart disease.

You may walk instead of ride, give up eating meat for a diet of grains, legumes, fruit and vegetables, you may be careful with calories – but yet, die a victim of negative emotions.

Experiencing brutality or observing it may induce similar behavior in the observer, particularly if the observer is immature. It is a confirmed observation that abused children have an increased probability of becoming child abusers.

Do the educators and propagandists who have promoted the forceful projection of scenes of horror with accompanying auditory input not expect effects upon the unconscious as well as the conscious minds of children or even adults? Add some suggestions of sexual arousal and the impression goes deeper.

Many people voice or write of their concern for the effect on the young of words and acts, of sounds and sights of cruel and destructive acts on radio and TV. According to the National Coalition on Television Violence there are more than 700 studies and reports on TV violence. They are overwhelming in their conclusion that a direct and major causal connection to real-life violence exists. Dr. Hollenbach of the National Institutes of Mental Health said that this may be the best proven fact in the whole field of psychology.

Could this be the factor society was missing in trying to understand the aberrant behavior in Hicksville and Hebron?

In Los Angeles, jail officials reported continuing anger and racial conflict from televised images three years after the 1992 riots that followed the first verdict in the Rodney King case. "Those images showed black rioters beating Hispanic men and women, along with whites, in the first hours of violence. These tapes were played over and over again, and people were getting more and more angry about it," said Paul Myron, Chief of the Custody Division of the Los Angeles County Sheriff's Department (*NYT* 6 F. 1995, A13).

What are the major messages repeated in the media relating to violence to people of African or Jewish descent? For the former, there is a constant stream of fiction and dramatic enactment of oppression and discrimination suffered by "minorities." For Jews, the major impact must be from the repeated forms of presentation of "the Holocaust." That these are powerful instruments producing emotional reactions in white people and in non-Jews is evident. There have been street demonstrations of thousands in major cities of western Europe by Europeans against "racism," and by non-Jews against "anti-Semitism" when a synagogue or Jewish graveyard has been desecrated.[*] In the United States, we have had riots and street

---

[*]   Oleg Kalugin, former Chief of counterintelligence and Major General K.G.B, wrote of his "active measures" campaign in the United States, that seems to have been copied in Germany and France. The campaign included the writing of "anti-Semitic letters to American Jewish leaders. My fellow officers paid American agents to paint swastikas on synagogues in New York and Washington. Our New York people even hired people to desecrate several Jewish cemeteries. I, of course, beamed back reports of these

demonstrations on occasions relating to experiences of these two groups. If strong emotions of empathy and anger are evoked in whites and non-Jews by the stimuli of these presentations of anti-"minority" and "anti-Semitic" violence, how must "minorities" and Jews feel?

According to his landlord, Ferguson blamed racism for all his misfortunes and shattered expectations. Some Jews could but feel revulsion "when they heard some neighbors of the settler, Dr. Baruch Goldstein, gloat over what a gift he had handed them for the Jewish holiday of Purim" (*NYT*. 27 Feb. 1994 A1:4). Goldstein, one may speculate, killed and died under the burden of the Holocaust, of *Schindler's List*, and all that has gone before it. Goldstein's emotions were not unique, but shared by a sensitized minority. Dov Lior, chief rabbi of the 6,000 strong Jewish settlement of Kiryat Arba, eulogized Goldstein as a "martyr" whose memory should be revered by Jews similar to those of victims of the Holocaust.

More Jews are becoming aware of how psychologically damaging repetition of the "holocaust" story is to their people. Rabbi Eli Hecht wrote in *The Los Angeles Times* Jan. 2, 1994 an article "When Will Jews Let it Rest?" "I am sick and tired of this generation identifying Judaism with suffering. Why is it imperative for our children and young people to visit Holocaust museums? Why do they need to hear lectures about skinheads and neo-Nazis and growing anti-Semitism? Why should they see every film about the Holocaust, always portraying Jews as victims running for their lives?"

Speaking of Israeli psychological resistance to moving forward in peacemaking with the Palestinians, Communications Minister Shulamit Aloni told a radio interviewer on March 24, 1994, "...we have got to get it into our heads once and for all that in our relations with the Palestinians we are not the victims. We are the rulers; we are the occupiers."

There is an African-American tradition of pride in self-help rather than self-pity, of looking forward, from Booker T. Washington, Marcus Garvey, W.E.B. DuBois and Elijah Muhammed, to some leaders today. But in contemporary America, "It was hammered into the African-American psyche by media-

---

misdeeds to my listeners in Moscow" (Kalugin, Oleg. *The First Directorate*, N.Y.: St. Martin's, 1994, pp. 52-3).

appointed black leaders and the white media that it was essential to our political progress to stay or seem to stay economically and socially deprived," writes Leonce Gaiter from Los Angeles. "To be recognized and recognize oneself as middle or upper class was to threaten the political progress of black people."

"Imagine being told by your peers, the records you hear, the programs you watch, the 'leaders' you see on TV, classmates, prospective employers – imagine being told by virtually everyone that in order to be your true self you must be ignorant and poor, or at least seem so" (*The New York Times Magazine* 28 June 1994, p.43).

What did Ferguson and Goldstein have in common?

Forget Brooklyn!

It was probably chronic anger and rage. Rage so great that they felt compelled to take it out on others. The constant repetition of the violence expressed in the audiovisual and written materials on Afro-American slavery and on the Holocaust, a Niagara of negativism, must have an effect upon the psyches of recipients. It may be experienced as violation – as violence. It is a form of torture of the psyche; which may produce distortions of perception and judgment, a tendency to delusions of persecution or grandiosity, focused or generalized anxiety or fear and or depression. There is psychological projection on to others of self-experience. Their hatred, projected on to others, made them believe that others hated them. This is not to excuse these murderers, but to explain them.

From University of California School of Social Ecology, Psychology and Social Behavior, Raymond. W. Novaco notes [*Behavior Change*, 1993, Vol. 10(4), 208-218] that contextually, anger is commonly represented as being due to acute, proximate occurrences. However, clinicians are urged to be aware of anger or rage as sometimes being slow-burning, and fueled over a period. It may be a product of contextual conditions that may involve distal determinants.

Could those who have written or produced so many dramas on the horrors of slavery and its aftermaths have had a part in the mind-set of Colin Ferguson as he set out for Hicksville on his mission of death? Were Stephen Spielberg's images from *Schindler's List* a last straw on many of the Holocaust that overburdened Baruch Goldstein?

Many African-Americans and Israelis are sorely in need of liberation from their constant toxic dict of mental violence, victimology, and negative thinking. We need to liberate ourselves from the pervasive false guilt, psychological flagellation, oppression, violence and negativism of Slavery and Holocaust.

Who supplies this diet? Where are the toxic ingredients mixed? They mostly come from "Hollywood." The Hollywood oligarchy that controls the production and distribution of "motion pictures" employs a group of a few hundred writers who produce about ninety percent of the ideas and scripts that end up being fed to the American people on film and TV, and exported to the rest of the world, especially Western Europe.

At a meeting of the International Society for Traumatic Stress Studies at the American Red Cross in New York in May 1994, a psychologist and former member of the Israeli army, spoke on psychological "Trauma, Integration and Healing." A psychiatrist questioned her on the possible psychological trauma to children who are exposed to portrayals of "The Holocaust," at ages when they are cognitively unable to assess and analyze the significance of the horror and violence in the events and details. She was taken aback, saying that no one had ever raised the question of a harmful or traumatic effect of teaching on the Holocaust. She worked on the curriculum of Holocaust studies for schoolchildren in New Jersey, she said, and would never do anything to harm children. Reaching for a coherent reply she said, "Some of the teachers of the program are better therapists than therapists." She blurted this out with a pressure of speech of considerable inner emotional investment. The audience of a couple of hundred was pin-drop quiet. Legislators who have voted for these studies as "politically correct," and parents who accept them: Who would harm your children for their own purposes?

To take an extreme possibility, who can say that the increase in white juvenile suicides may not be related to the now widespread projection of the "Holocaust" and racial violence into American schools, and its introjection into immature minds, as used to happen with nuclear catastrophe "morning-after" presentations. Increasing numbers of African American leaders are coming to believe that anti-social behavior by their teenagers may be at least partly a result of negative input. James Farmer, director of the Congress of Racial Equality, who believes in legal equality, is one of them.

Do the educators and propagandists who have promoted the forceful projection of scenes of horror with accompanied auditory input not expect effects upon the unconscious as well as the conscious minds of children? Could the children who got special attention from authorities for laughing during obligatory viewing of *Schindler's List* not be trying to relieve their tension and anxiety? Following the incident, 16,000 Californian students a week "studied the Holocaust for at least two hours before attending private screenings of 'Schindler's List' at local theaters" (*NYT.* 13 Ap. 1994, B11:1). Black youths may use weapons, drugs or pregnancy and procreation to assert their independence from authority, which is associated with oppression in the messages that the system gives them. And white children have guilt instilled into them in school and church – for slavery, and for the deaths of Jews in concentration camps.

This sickens the spirit. Do not support it in the classroom, at the box office, with your television. It is appropriate to repeat the following.

Guilt is – in a sense – a self-administered punishment. False guilt is unlimited self-punishment. With false guilt – the Western sickness of the end of the century – comes depression. Attempts at expiation of false guilt do not lift the depression. They become a self-destructive psychopathology.

> And so in the Libyan fable, it is told
> That once an eagle, stricken with a dart
> Said when he saw the fashion of the shaft
> With our own feathers, not by other hands
> Are we now stricken! — AESCHYLUS

In 1994, on the 25th anniversary of the Sunday in 1969 when Neil Armstrong and Edwin Aldrin landed on the moon in the Eagle spacecraft and became the first humans to walk on another celestial body, Mr. Aldrin spoke to a meeting of astronauts, Congressmen and aerospace industry executives.

"For one crowning moment we were creatures of the cosmic ocean, a moment that a thousand years hence may be seen as the signature of our century," Mr. Aldrin said. *"Yet an eerie apathy now seems to inflict the very generation who witnessed and were inspired by those events."*

This is consistent with our diagnosis that there is a malaise of the spirit in the Western world, that now two centuries of optimism, progress and order are ending. The malaise and stultification of the development of the Western tradition, are consequences of the milieu of cultural confusion, or multiculturalism, with the suppression of free inquiry and report, and the imposition and introjection of spurious guilt.

Garrett Hardin, Professor Emeritus of Human Ecology at the University of California at Santa Barbara, led a counter-attack on the evil empire of contemporary sociopolitical irrationality with his essay on "The Tragedy of the Commons" (*Science*, 162 1968). In his 1993 book, *Living Within Limits: Ecology, Economics and Population Taboos* (Oxford, 1993, p.306), he records:

> Anyone who tries to comprehend the spirit of our times is soon impressed with the popularity of guilt-mongering – making other people feel guilty about something....

In an interview before leaving his post as director of the National Institutes of Mental Health in 1994 to found a center on science, medicine and human values at George Washington University, Frederick K. Goodwin M.D. (with an excellent record of research on the biology of depression) said, "In the last generation, we've seen a doubling of the suicide rate, the doubling of depression, the doubling of the divorce rate, 50 percent decline in parenting time, increased crimes of violence. A whole series of larger social trends - which might be called an unraveling of the way in which people used to develop...we used to have a patriotic identity, a neighborhood identity, an ethnic identity, religious identity, and identity with two parents with extended family....Scientists have avoided values because they think values have to mean religion, and I don't think they do."

Evolutionary biology and advances in cognitive science, offer insights to value systems that maximize our quality of life and continuity. Just as our hands and eyes have been formed by millions of years of evolutionary history, so the information processing systems of our minds have developed systems of behavior, and social and environmental reactions. An evolutionary approach begins with understanding the principle of adaptation. Adaptations evolved through natural selection to increase the probability of survival of an individual's genes. For example, common causes of nausea and vomiting are toxic substances, and the symptoms tend to cause us to expel them and reject them in the future. In their

1995 book *Why We Get Sick: The New Science of Darwinian Medicine*, R. Nesse and G. Williams show how in every branch of medicine - infectious disease, oncology, psychiatry - "medical research and practice would be even better if questions of adaptation and historical causation [evolutionmary explanations] were routinely considered along with those of immediate physical and chemical causation," or "proximate explanations." Proximate explanations answer questions of "what" and "how" about structure and mechanisms; evolutionary explanations answer questions about origins and functions.

We live in a Sentimental Society. We do not want to face life as it really is at all. We don't want people to die. We torture people by putting tubes into them when they are very old and frail, and really the time has come for them to die. We strive officiously to keep alive fetuses with multiple deformities, without regard for their quality of life. We are out of touch with nature. We need to understand what values are related to society in terms of its needs, and what values are biologically based. Take the biblical value which is still used by many orthodox Jews and Roman Catholics, "Be fruitful and multiply." That had a social value, it had a survival value at another time, in certain places. But for the people of Iberoamerica, is that a value which enhances their quality of life? And if you take those people out of that situation and you say come to this place or that place with a lower population density and a better probability of survival, you separate people from the consequences of their acts. Does intervening between social cause and effect not tend to destroy the development of autonomy? That is what many people do.

A Healthy Body

A European visitor to the U.S.A. was taken to see a football game at the University of Iowa, and afterwards invited to tour the locker and changing rooms. His impressions of American football are not relevant here, although the huge modern investment of time and resources in the contemporary equivalent of Roman circuses is socially significant. He was surprised to see that all the men had been circumcised.

In a previous chapter the mutilations called female circumcision was mentioned in relation to the custom of some non-European immigrants. Female circumcision or removal of the clitoral prepuce is a standard procedure among many Moslems. Excision of the clitoris, a resection of the labia minora, in Arabic *khefdz* - planing, is common throughout Moslem Africa, the Middle East and Southeast Asia. The age of choice, from a few weeks to several years, depends upon the area.

But how many Americans resist this barbaric custom or ritual being performed on their infant boys? Proponents of circumcision defend it with various arguments of prophylaxis, for example.[*] But it is a mutilation, painful, and not without resulting disability. Localized pain and discomfort in an infant may predispose to sexual problems, reduction of sensitivity and increase in sexual aggressivity in an adult.

Opposed to this genital abuse, and all other mutilations and exaggerations, including massive muscle-building, is the classical ideal of beauty of the healthy developed balanced body – unmutilated, unscarified, and for men - unpierced. Those were barbarian customs. The march of the Ten Thousand eastwards in 400 B.C., told in Xenophon's *Anabasis*, includes a soldier being dismissed for wearing earrings like a Lydian. At one time in imperial Rome, performing circumcision on a Roman could be punishable by death. In our society, it could be punishable by litigation. The circumcised and their sexual partners lose far more than a foreskin.

In other chapters we have had to deal with the negative forces in religions, economics, politics, with history, because the knowledge is needed to free us from the thought control system that otherwise deleteriously effects our minds and behavior. In the matter of the healthy body, we can effect self improvement, within limitations of our heredity, and environment that we can try to improve.

James Hervey Johnson was a non-drinker, non-smoker, a vegetarian. He enjoyed walking, often south from San Diego. A nutritious balanced healthy diet, exercise, and loving something outside oneself, are requisites for health. He believed that eating fruits nuts and vegetables, especially dark-green, yellow-orange and red ones like spinach, papaya, carrots, sweet potatoes, winter squash, apricots, cantaloupes, tomatoes and red peppers, are

---

[*] The preputially disadvantaged seek justification for their difference but, for example, statistics collected during a 15-year period confirm that the incidence of cervical cancer among native Turkish women is as frequent as among the Western and non-Moslem non-Jewish women in Turkey (Eser, S. *Brit. M. J.* 5416:1073-4).

exposition. Johnson's dedication to the "outside oneself" is continued in this work. You may share in it by publicizing the ideas in this book.

Aldrin's gloomy comparison has a faint reflection from the thought of the medieval philosopher John of Salisbury. Looking back to men like the Greek philosopher Protagoras who believed, "Man is the measure of all things," John declared, "We are dwarfs, standing on the shoulders of giants." John was living in a culture of religion that taught that "Only Man is vile," and also with the dialectic that Man was made in the image of God. John looked back to the light.

But a new humanism was ahead when republican Florence would be compared to Athens in the age of Pericles, and the architect Leon Battista Alberti addressed his fellow man in these words: "To you is given a body more graceful than other animals, to you power of apt and various movements, to you most sharp and delicate sense, to you wit, reason, memory like an immortal god." Florence looked back to look to itself. We should look back to look to ourselves to look to the future.

Kenneth Clark described the library of San Marco, built by Cosimo de Medici to house and study ancient texts, "as the humanist equivalent of the Cavendish Laboratory" (*Civilization.* 1969, 93), where Lord Rutherford demonstrated the path of an electron for the first time. The simple cloud chamber was a result of the experimental method, and his saying: "We haven't much money. We'll have to use our brains." The germinal element of the Renaissance compares with the electron basis of the nuclear and information age.

Is it relevant to the state of our spirit that for half a century, literally measuring Man has been more than a little like the fearsome tasks of celestial measurements and heretical questionings of religious dogma in medieval Europe? We have had Inquisitors and official doctrine - and Galileos, while the world was largely in ignorance of the struggle for free inquiry, or told to dismiss the persecuted as extremists.

You may use a computer, but the Inquisitions are shadows of the Dark Side of a Dark Age. Yet, may some of us look ahead to a New Enlightenment? Its realization depends upon you.

7

MEASURING MAN
What Difference Does it Make?

After viewing a balloon ascent in Paris in 1782, Benjamin Franklin immediately wrote off about it to his friends at the Royal Society in London. And to the inevitable question from an onlooker: "But what use is it?" He made the irresistible reply: *"What use is a baby."*

When I showed the previous chapters of this book manuscript to a lawyer, a man of unusual integrity, he confirmed what I already knew: that the mindset or prejudice of some readers would probably pigeonhole this book in a "racist" category, although its underlying theme is an exposure of religion as against reason. I replied that our position did not fit Andrew Huxley's definition of belief in the rule of one race over another, and we believed the old arguments of "superior" and "inferior" to be sterile. But we do believe that there are racial differences.

He replied, "But what difference does it make?" And he asked me if I had read *The Mismeasure of Man* by S. J. Gould.

That recalled an experience some years ago when I read in one of Stephen J. Gould's stimulating *influential* articles in *Natural History*, published by the American Museum of Natural History, that there was no appreciable difference in brain size between races – "as if that mattered."

I had recently read of some considerable research done by an East Asian pathologist in Milwaukee on brain weight in relation to sex, race and age, in a somewhat obscure journal (Ho, Khang-cheng. Arch. Pathol. Lab. Med. Vol. 104, Dec. 1980, 635-44), that demonstrated statistically significant differences. Knowing that I had come across the reference by chance, and that such data may be missed by a biologist, I sent a copy of the report to the editor of *Natural History* asking him to send it to Professor Gould, with a very simple letter with the reference for publication of record. There was no response. Following my inquiry, the editor wrote that publication of my letter had been considered, but eventually rejected because Gould had written that there were no "appreciable" differences. That is what advertising people call "weasel wording." The differences were statistically significant at a certain level of confidence. The results could be confirmed or not by further studies, but not otherwise ignored, according to the scientific method in general use.

I mentioned this experience to the lawyer on the telephone. Then I said that in my files was a picture of the contestants in the 100-meter race at the European games. All were African! If one were an athlete that could be important. He said, "There's a basketball game on my television. All the players are black."

Arguably, knowledge has generally been politicized throughout our history; but objectivity increases the probability of discovery and positive change. Change or revision in history has a value in straightening distortions, so that its lessons may be better understood and manipulations for ulterior motives reduced. Objectivity to use new knowledge or analysis offers opportunity for change in society's socio-political and economic actions so that they are more in accord with observation, and more likely to produce the promoted result. Educated in the pre-World War II classical liberal tradition that persisted for a while after it, one finds it hard to understand why people may not prefer knowledge, even "for the sake of knowing."

To share another experience … When the epidemic spread of AIDS became a fact of life in American cities, I was working in a state hospital that served an inner city area where risk factors were high; but physicians were barred by state policy from asking for HIV tests unless suspicious symptoms had developed. At a medical staff meeting, I offered a motion recommending to the state health commissioner and legislature the routine testing of admissions for HIV, just as was done for syphilis. To my surprise, the opposition was preponderantly against the idea, with the argument that a positive result could lead to "discrimination" against patients who had tested positive. Only when AZT was introduced as a drug that could retard the development of AIDS was the policy changed. I simply believed one could not know too much about a patient under one's care and responsibility.

What the lawyer brought to my immediate attention was that an educated concerned person in our society may have no inkling of the knowledge that is available on race differences, and that the potential importance of some of them is increasingly recognized. I find retracing my steps a little boring but it is instructive. Please follow me.

Years ago, I spent several years in writing and historical research. Eventually, with my savings exhausted, I looked for a part-time job and found one in a blood bank that left me free to start writing in the afternoon. Occasionally, I would hear some of the urban poor clientele – largely blacks and occasionally American Indians – often interesting people, who got five dollars a pint – ask the management personnel whether their blood was "different." The invariable reply was that blood was all the same. One day I questioned the woman who said this as she was labeling a batch of bloods. Apart from blood type, I pointed out to her, it was so apparent that hardly any two pints she was labeling even looked alike. There was a wide range of color of the plasma and its apparent opacity, and in the appearance of the packed red cells. She had to agree, but had not really thought about it before.

After my project was finished, I accepted an assignment to review an investigation set up by a company on a new agent to treat constipation. It was a suppository that was being compared with a control glycerin suppository in the maternity wards of a hospital in Jacksonville, Florida. The study was being run by a research nurse who made all the observations herself. When the results were analyzed statistically, it was found that the new product worked better than the control. But of the four wards, it worked significantly faster in two than in the other two. Why? I was asked to find out. Finding: the wards were segregated, and the results in the two black ones were different from the two white ones. The product was never marketed. The company had no further interest in the study and it was never published. I was interested.

I began to review the literature for race differences. When I had enough for publication, I passed the file to a medical writer who made abstracts of the reports, classified them and so on. He divided the differences according to epidemiology or incidence of disease, anatomical differences, physiological response, biochemistry, and cultural response differences. In brief, publishers distanced themselves from me. I continued collecting, at one time paying graduate students to help, but discontinued systematic collecting years ago, since I could put the results to no use. Did the differences matter?

Let me offer a few samples from each section from more than thirty years ago.

Ethic Derivation as Related to Cancer at various Sites.

Ethnic Distribution of Diabetes.
Extremes of Coronary Heart Disease in Ethnic Groups in Johannesburg.
Racial, Age and Regional Differences in Human Sebaceous glands in the Head and Neck.
Variations in Axillary Odor.
Buoyancy as Predicted by Certain Anthropometric Measurements.
The Soft Anatomy of a North American Indian.

Thermal and Metabolic Responses of Coastal Eskimos During a Cold Night.
Natural State of Heat Acclimatization of Different Ethnic Groups.
Physiological Regulation in Moist Heat by Young American Negro And White Males.
Racial Differences in Skin Resistance.
Racial Group Differences in the Basal Metabolism and Body Composition of Indian and European Women in Bombay.

Serum Uric Acid Levels of Healthy Caucasian, Chinese and Haida Indian in British Columbia.
Differences in Serum Cholesterol in Young Adult White Males and Negro Adults.
The Natural History of Aortic Atherosclerosis: Relationship to Race, Sex, and Coronary Lesions in New Orleans.
Further Observations on Trimodality of Frequency Distribution Curve of Biologically Active Isoniazid Blood Levels and "Cline" in Frequencies of Alleles Controlling Isoniazid Activation.

School Leaving Due to Pregnancy in an Urban Adolescent Population.
Cultural Bias of Psychological Test Items.
Rise in Frequency of Suicide.

Did any of these data matter? The answer is obvious to me.

Our next stop is in the late 1970s when I started to study Psychiatry. At our first lecture on Alcoholism, the lecturer made no mention of the difference in metabolism of alcohol by Europeans and American Indians. Questioning the lecturer, I found he was unaware of the literature on the subject. So I brought a copy of a published study to his next lecture. It showed that Amerindians do not metabolize ethyl alcohol as easily as Europids, so that toxic pyruvate levels build up in the blood, impairing judgment to a much greater degree that would generally occur with a white person ingesting the same quantity of alcohol. Yet everyone has heard of the tragic effects of "fire water" on the native Indians in American history. Indians were despised when they could not "hold their liquor." Do these data matter?

Incidentally, on heredity, the data on the heritability of certain types of alcohol addiction, of mental illness and personality disorder, was becoming too voluminous to be ignored, as was the topic in the general media, except to be associated with German National Socialism and the "holocaust," and discredited as a pseudo-science. In psychiatry, the data were treated as a rather new area. When we discussed manic-depressive illness, the American literature's first reference I was told was about 1955. At our journal club, I was able to quote the study of Eliot Slater published in the *Proceedings of the Royal Society of Medicine* in 1936 (29:981-90). He had done the work at the Research Institute for Psychiatry in Munich in 1934-35, based on the records of 315 probands with recurrent illnesses, their parents and their children. Presumably the prejudice against its time and place of origin, and heredity as a factor of importance in Medicine, had consigned the work to oblivion in the United States. I had met Slater years before and went to see him in retirement in 1980 after I became a psychiatrist, as he had said I would become one when he first met me. His Selected Papers in Psychiatry and Genetics were published as a tribute or *festschrift* by Johns Hopkins as *Man, Mind, and Heredity* in 1971. (Progress in knowledge of heredity, conducted over decades at the Minnesota Center for Twin and Adoption Research and in Europe, is generally unreported or distorted in media – another instance of suppression of information relevant to our survival.)

I wished that I could introduce anti-abortionists to women who had several children in foster care and were pregnant, hospitalized because of mental illness so severe that they were a danger to themselves or others. Abortion? No. Foster care again? No, "this time I'm going to keep my baby," they would say; although they were unable to care for themselves.

When I became a professor and started teaching medical students, I had to mention racial differences. Why? Here is a quotation from *Psychiatric Times* (Mr. 1995, 22).

Ethnic differences in pharmacodynamics have long been reported in terms of responses to mydriatics (Garde and others 1978) and beta-blockers (Moser and Lunn 1981). Recent studies by Zhou and colleagues (1989) objectively stated that the effects of propanalol (Inderal) on blood pressure and heart rate were most pronounced in Asians, and least prominent in African-Americans, with Caucasians falling between (Dimsdale and others 1988; Rutledge and colleagues 1989). Observations of the ethnic differences in therapeutic concentrations of various psychotropics (Hu and coworkers 1983; Takahashi 1979; Yamashita and Asano 1979) and their neurohormonal effects have led to speculation about the ethnic differences in pharmacodynamics of these drugs.

Do racial differences matter? At the 1994 annual meeting of the National Medical Association, the African American equivalent of the American Medical Association, a keynote speaker stressed the need for more research that specifically studied their people. Is this racism, prejudice, bigotry?

"Doctors are showing a cautious resurgence of interest in giving more consideration to their patients' racial or ethnic backgrounds when diagnosing or treating illnesses.

"Mounting evidence suggests that race and ethnicity can and should be factors in evaluating symptoms while reaching a diagnosis and in determining the treatment and how the patients fare.

"Because of the country's sensitivity to racial issues, there has been a reluctance to address race or ethnicity in medicine except in the most obvious cases, experts say. Tay-Sachs disease among descendants of Eastern European Jews, sickle-cell disease and hypertension among blacks, diabetes among some native Americans, and stomach cancer among immigrant Asians are well-known conditions associated with particular groups. But specialists note that other well-known health problems, although often considered ethnically neutral, may express themselves in different ways and vary in incidence among ethnic groups, requiring different approaches in treatment."

Those three paragraphs are from the Science section of the *New York Times* (25 S. 1990, C10). I can remember when publishing data on Tay-Sach's disease and Amaurotic idiocy among Ashkenazic Jews was denounced as anti-Semitic;[*] then came amniocentesis – like Azt.

---

[*] My late friend Benjamin H. Freedman, of German-Jewish origin, used to publish such material and was denounced as anti-Semitic by the Anti-Defamation League of Bnai Brith. He believed that there was a preponderance of psychological instability among

Nature has developed multiple levels of interaction. To quote J. Gould, "Selection does not only sort organisms, as Darwin thought; it operates simultaneously at several levels of genealogical hierarchy – on genes and cell lineages 'below' organisms and species 'above' organisms" (*Natural History* 7/92). The American anthropologist Carleton Coon,[**] who was vilified and then rehabilitated, like Burt, pointed out that the differences in odor between human races suggested the advanced development of speciation. Is it not hubris to end this multi-millennial process forever in one or two generations when our knowledge of evolutionary processes is still so rudimentary?

We support the integrity of tribal, racial or national ethnic groups; for differentiation is part of biological and cultural evolution. Powerful economic and political forces are used to try to erase these differences through various forms of disintegration of natural communities.

A right, even of *cultural* continuity, is beginning to be recognized; it should consciously be part of legislative and legal decisions, and planning for the future. An example of such a legal recognition of a right of ethnic cultural identity comes from Scotland. A ruling at the Court of Sessions in Edinburgh (10 Mr. 1995) allowed a Scottish couple to adopt two Asian children provided, "The petitioners shall use their best endeavours to secure that the children will be made aware of their black identity and brought up with an understanding of their ethnic origin and tradition."[***] Wearing a kilt does not make an Asian into a Scot. Psychological denial would have it otherwise.

Jews from Eastern Europe and Russia, and there seems to be some supporting evidence in Israeli studies.

[**] Coon promulgated a multiregional hypothesis in which racial differences were attributed to races emerging at different times in evolutionary history, with distinctive physiological characteristics and adaptations to climate and temperature.

[***] Adoptive parents tend to psychological denial of the adoptive child's differences from them. Increasingly, adopted children seek a natural parent to learn more about their inherited physical and psychological characteristics. Children of sociopathic parents may exhibit such characteristics however much tender loving care they are given, and murder of adoptive 'parents' by such adoptees is not uncommon.

Turn the question around. What are the motivations of those who promote the dissolution of ethnic or racial differences? Who wants to assimilate the American Indian and the natives of the rain forests? If it is for a more peaceful world, that is plainly fallacious. Civil wars have been the most bitter and bloody. It is grandiose: a belief that one knows so surely the cause of ethnic conflict as to advocate an irrevocable solution.

Such equalists seldom keep up with the literature: who can, and does? For example a basic argument of Susan Olzak (*The Dynamics of Competition and Conflict*. Stanford, 1992) is that competition is the driving mechanism behind most ethnic conflict. She challenges previous theories that suggest that ethnic conflict arises from things like relative deprivation, modernization and development, and assimilation difficulties that result in threats to an existing ethnically defined balance of power. One of her primary hypotheses, supported by observations, is that ethnic conflict arises not from the separation and relative deprivation of groups, but rather from the breakdown of the former social order that kept the groups apart. It is when groups mix that they begin to compete. Essentially, they compete for the same limited resources, and Olzak's perspective is like that of a population biologist who sees much of the world in terms of competing species.

The evolution of form modified by function is a mega process of life. D'Arcy Thompson traced appreciation of the concept to the late seventeenth century and commented:

> Organic form is found, mathematically speaking, to be a function of time.... We might call the form of an organism an event in *space-time*, and not merely a configuration space (*On Growth and Form*, 1952).

Researchers who study why animals are attracted to each other, and why a face or figure may be alluring, have gathered evidence that symmetry of form is an underlying factor. This, in turn, is a reasonably reliable indicator of quality. Writing in the January 1994 issue of the journal *Trends in Ecology and Evolution*, P. Watson and R. Thornhill sum up data gathered on the role of symmetry in mate selection. "The individuals who have had a good developmental background come out more symmetrical," said Dr. Thornhill. "They are put together better and they will do better in competition for resources and mates." These are among the many factors we are only beginning to measure. Should we not be careful not to change things we do not understand? Nature and nurture over millennia have produced the different life forms we see around us including human races and further ethnic divisions. Shall we, in a handful of generations negate those diversities, and move humanity towards entropy?

Mimicking Evolution: The Emergence of Complex Forms

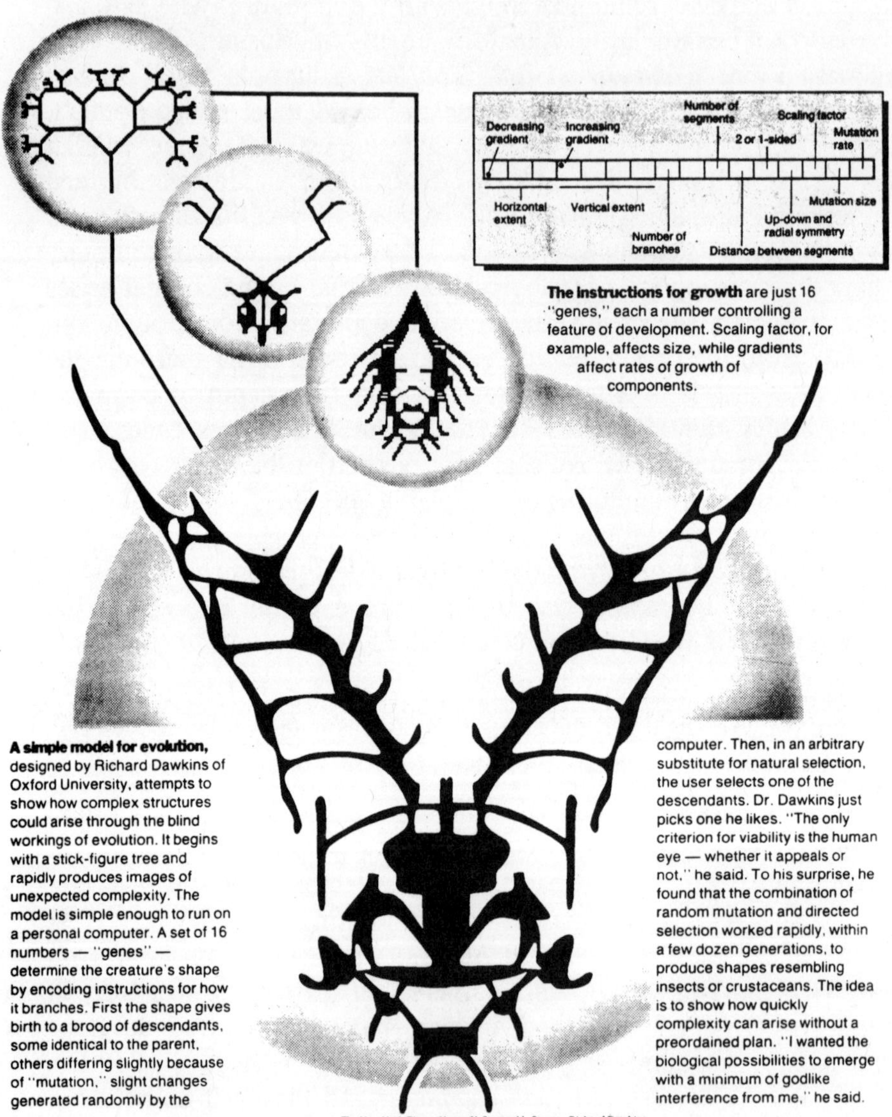

The instructions for growth are just 16 "genes," each a number controlling a feature of development. Scaling factor, for example, affects size, while gradients affect rates of growth of components.

A simple model for evolution, designed by Richard Dawkins of Oxford University, attempts to show how complex structures could arise through the blind workings of evolution. It begins with a stick-figure tree and rapidly produces images of unexpected complexity. The model is simple enough to run on a personal computer. A set of 16 numbers — "genes" — determine the creature's shape by encoding instructions for how it branches. First the shape gives birth to a brood of descendants, some identical to the parent, others differing slightly because of "mutation," slight changes generated randomly by the computer. Then, in an arbitrary substitute for natural selection, the user selects one of the descendants. Dr. Dawkins just picks one he likes. "The only criterion for viability is the human eye — whether it appeals or not," he said. To his surprise, he found that the combination of random mutation and directed selection worked rapidly, within a few dozen generations, to produce shapes resembling insects or crustaceans. The idea is to show how quickly complexity can arise without a preordained plan. "I wanted the biological possibilities to emerge with a minimum of godlike interference from me," he said.

The New York Times/Nancy Y. Sterngold; Source: Richard Dawkins

A conference on artificial life held at Los Alamos National Laboratory in 1987 brought together there for the first time models of processes from protein formation to plant growth to animal predation. The simulations of biology addressed some of the most challenging questions of the life sciences: how the primitive precursors of DNA gained the ability to store information and copy it; how the senseless force of natural selection created structures of such extraordinary complexity and what one may call beauty; how the laws of ecosystems originate from the behavior of individual animals. Richard Dawkins of Oxford University offered a simple model for evolution: The Emergence of Complex Forms (p.86).

The Los Alamos conference's competition for the most lifelike organism was won with a program that mimicked the growth of a variety of flower species. This program of Przemyslaw Prusinkiewicz of the University of Regina in Canada, using developmental algorithms of the late Aristide Lindenmayer of the University of Utrecht, combined geometric instructions with a set of timing signals, like the chemical signals that real plants use to control branching and budding. The results were vivid images of plant growth. Some of these are in their wonderful book *The Algorithmic Beauty of Plants* (1990, Springer). But Lindenmayer and his Dutch colleagues had written of "many growth processes of living organisms ..." including animals.

"If they don't have the whole enchilada, at least they have a few pieces of lettuce," said a computer columnist.

J. Doyne Farmer of Los Alamos, an expert on chaotic dynamics working on modeling the body's immune system, echoed some other scientists in calling the prospects frightening, perhaps not so much because of what might be created like a Frankenstein monster, as because of what it might tell us about people.

Homo res naturales est = Man is a thing of nature—Thomas Acquinas.

8

Is There Life Everlasting?

When the last individual of a race of living things breathes no more, another heaven and earth must pass before such a one can be again.—William Beebe. Quoted on a sign at Queens Zoo, New York, on a memorial to extinct local species.

If you suffered a concussion, there would probably be some degree of retrograde amnesia. As you regained consciousness, your first question would probably be:
Where am I?
Then, *How did I get here?*
And then, *What am I doing here?*

We cannot know when someone first asked the questions, or know who first asked them. The various religions have provided explanations the average person finds easy to relate to, or evangelists put them in terms acceptable to their audience. When offered consistently from infancy onwards, religious belief usually becomes the organizing factor in a person's view of themselves and their view of their relationship to the cosmos.

Where Am I?

Atlas holds up the earth. It is borne on the back of a great turtle, and so on. We do know that over two millennia ago, the earth was being considered in a way that we associate with Western thought and modern science. From the 5th century B.C. Ionian beginning of Western natural philosophy, philosophers with courage began to free us from the fear and caprice of imaginary gods and magic. About 580 B.C. Thales of Miletus speculated that life had not been created by the gods, but had emerged by natural means from water. By 260 B.C. Aristarchus of Samos understood that the earth revolved around the sun. Ten years later in Alexandria, Eratosthenes calculated the circumference of the earth within two hundred miles. There was a heliocentric cosmology.

Like some other empire builders and dreamers, Alexander the Great seems to have believed that by conquering barbarian peoples who did not speak Greek and extending Greek rule, the world he conquered would become like the Greece he knew. He encouraged the race-mixing of his soldiers with the peoples he conquered as far as the Punjab. Was the world he conquered Hellenized? It is wonderful and amazing to see in a now desolate part of Afghanistan, the ruins of an unmistakably Greek city.

Although Alexandria became a great center of learning, a result of those conquests and empire was the same as it has been for the European and American empires in our time. There have been massive influxes of immigrants from the empires into their centers. In Greece, the path of Greek thought began to change. Samos lost its liberty to an Athenian central authority. The result of Alexander's empire "was not cultural conformity but syncretism, cultural confusion, and the loss of cultural identity by native and immigrant alike. Not only were the cultures of the conquered territories 'syncretized' with Greek culture, but native Greek culture was gradually transformed and de-Hellenized" (Sociological Aspects of Religious Transformation in *The Germanization of Early Christianity*. Russell, J. Oxford: Oxford Univ. Press, 1994, p.85). So ended the glory that was Greece.

What has been called the "Hellenistic Enlightenment encouraged individualism and at the same time cosmopolitanism… But is was the Stoics who popularized the idea that all men are *cosmopolitai* – citizens of the same city, i.e., the cosmos – whatever their social origin or geographical situation" (*A History of Religious Ideas*. Eliade, M. Chicago: Chicago Univ. Press, 1982. vol. 2, .208.).

Cosmopolitanism brought a confusion of ideas and cosmologies. People whose ancestral roots were loosened were open to the appeal of mystery cults offering individual salvation and a renewed sense of community.

The same confusion of cosmologies and beliefs followed the extension of the Roman Empire. Later, when one asked, Where am I? the Abrahamic religions imposed the belief that Man and the earth were at the center, around which the sun, planets and celestial bodies revolved. This lasted for a Dark Age – until Copernicus.

In our lifetime, we have learnt – like children – our proper address. But unlike children, we were not told our address. We explored our surroundings with instruments we invented, developed, used – from the ruler to the telescope and the space ship.

We live in a solar system toward the edge of a major spiral galaxy, that we call the Milky Way. It is home to the sun and a few hundred billion other stars. The galaxy belongs in turn to a cluster of galaxies astronomers call the local group, and the local group is part of the Virgo super cluster, an archipelago of galaxies stretching across a hundred million light years of space.

How Did I get Here?

Once upon a time, a man in his early thirties set out on journey in the Tyrolean Alps. No one knows exactly what happened at 10,530 feet, but his body was found too late to revive him. He had frozen to death.

He died 5,300 years ago. He has been named Otzi, after the valley where he was found, although he was a Celt.

In June 1994 he was visited by his 200th generation descendant, Mrs. Marie Mosely, age 35. She is from Cork in Ireland and now lives comfortably with her husband in Bournemouth, Dorsetshire.

Scientists in Oxford, Munich, Zurich and Innsbruck made the connection after tracking a specific gene sequence identified from Otzi. By examining genetic material from 1,246 people across the world, the geneticists found the sequence did not occur in anyone from outside Europe. They also examined 72 people currently living in different parts of the Tyrol and found none of them carried it, although some northern Germans, Danes, Britons and Icelanders did.

Marie shares more genetic characteristics with Otzi than do any of the others who were examined. Whatever our race and ethnicity, there are behind us long lines of development that have made us what we are. Should we accept and act upon the unproved thesis offered to us by the power establishment that tells us that racial continuity, that ancestry, are matters of no importance? How do we know? Whatever we do is forever. Marie says, "I've decided not to have any children so it will be up to someone else to continue the ice family."

Which brings us to the last question of a person gaining consciousness.

What Am I Doing Here?

Myoho Renge Shu Buddhist philosophy teaches that the goal is *Peace of the Whole Universe, including Endless Future and Endless Dimensions*, to be attained through mankind's powerful chanting of Nam Myoho Renge Kyo to the mandala of HIKARI-DERA: the complete crystal of the true Buddha's endless Mercifulness. For Christians it is salvation for an afterlife.

In 1993 I was offered the facility of a friend's Gulfstream jet airplane to fly from New York to Los Angeles. Also on the $40 million plane with us was a Philippine maidservant and a personal secretary. During the flight I briefly joined them and the co-pilot in the rear of the plane. They were speaking with the maid who was telling them of her nine children, all working or married, with 22

Otzi the Ice Man

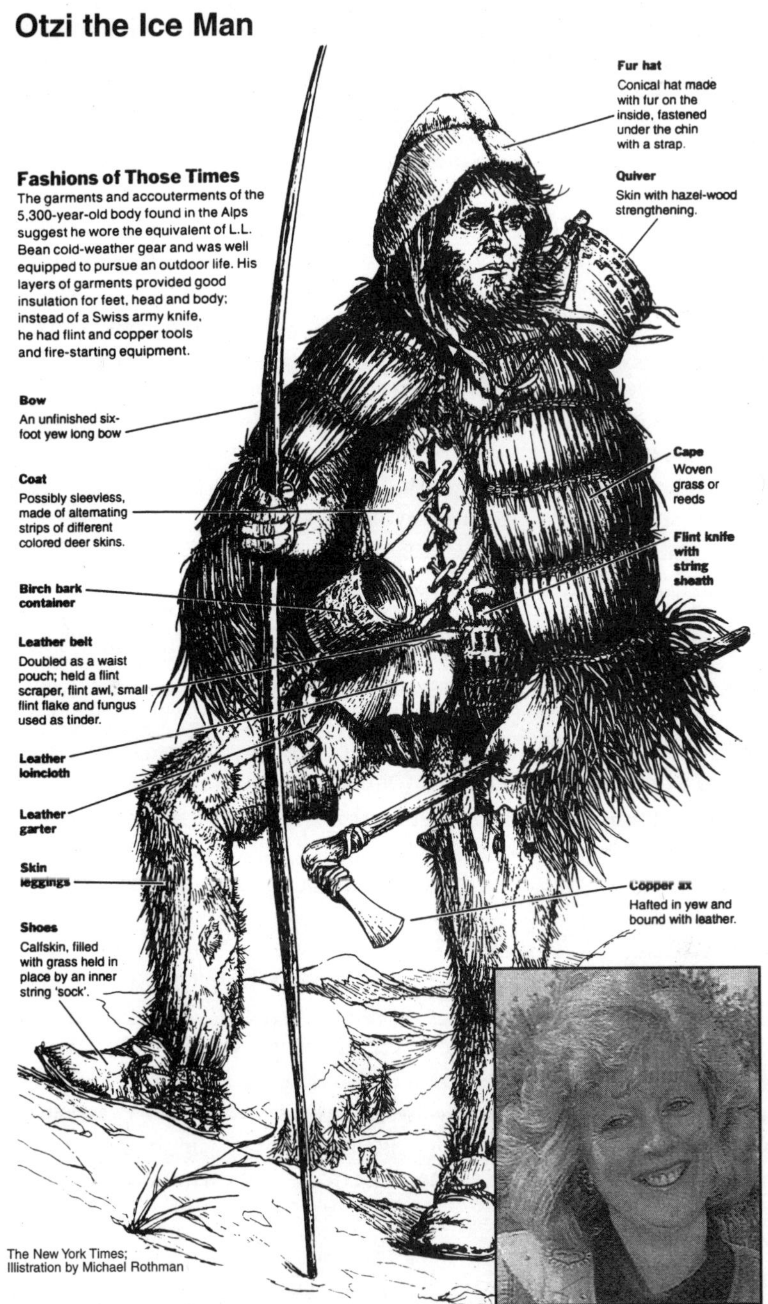

Fashions of Those Times

The garments and accouterments of the 5,300-year-old body found in the Alps suggest he wore the equivalent of L.L. Bean cold-weather gear and was well equipped to pursue an outdoor life. His layers of garments provided good insulation for feet, head and body; instead of a Swiss army knife, he had flint and copper tools and fire-starting equipment.

The New York Times;
Illistration by Michael Rothman

Marie: looking up an ancestor

children of their own. The co-pilot and secretary smiled with words and gestures of approbation. When she left us for a moment, I mentioned to the two of them how much more biologically successful was Rosa than any of us, for all our intelligence and education. They seemed to "sober up," and became serious and interested. The concept was new to them but is elementary to biology. I did not quote from E.O. Wilson's *On Human Nature*: "The human mind is a device for survival and reproduction, and reason is just one of its techniques."[*]

We are biodegradable but our genes can go marching on. Our characteristics can have life everlasting. It is not life that is sacred. It is the continuity of life and form.

This is part of our understanding of elementary biology and Darwinian theory.

Marie is a member of the middle class. Marie is a biological failure. Is she using the technique of reason? Biological success – measured by the number of progeny and their probability of survival and reproduction – is nature's success and the next step in time.

Working with social insects, W. D. Hamilton realized that if individuals within a group help one another, and they are genetically related, those genes they share will be passed on to the next generation, even if some of the individuals are sterile, such as worker ants or bees. This led him and others to realize that genes themselves are selected, as Richard Dawkins later described in *The Selfish Gene*. This insight led to a much clearer understanding why so many animals are social, for one of the advantages of group togetherness is genetic. A result has been the great surge since the 1970s in the study of Sociobiology, conveyed to the world by E. O. Wilson in his book of that name.

With the insight of Sociobiology, we can allow that there are rare individuals who do not themselves reproduce, who confer so much benefit on those who carry most of their genetic inheritance that their lives are a "group success;" those who stayed behind to give more time for their families to escape from invader, or the sacrifice of warriors like Leonidas, the heritage of Isaac Newton. Those who serve to support their people in lesser ways can

---

[*] All social animals - not just humans, make sharp significant distinctions between themselves and everyone else. For those who do not think biologically, consider a reproductive strategy of chimpanzees, with whom we share 97 percent similar DNA. When an alpha male is defeated, his successor will generally try to kill as many of his predecessor's progeny as possible. Also, the Mosaic tribal practice: "And they warred against the Midianites, as the Lord commanded Moses; and they slew all the males...But all the female children that have not known a man by lying with him, keep alive for yourselves" (Numbers 31:, 18).

conceivably confer group benefit also, in rare cases, an individual or group action can improve success for all humanity, or even all living things.

In *The Times* of London, 21 June 1994, three days after Marie's story, the review of a book appeared: *Motherhood Deferred: A Woman's Journey* (Putnam, 1994) by Anne Fleming. She describes herself as part of the "sacrificial generation" of women born in the 1950s. Along with millions of women of European origin, her life was coincidental with the rise of the radical part of the feminist movement. She became a full-time writer, putting the attainment of career success before biological success. She postponed having children until her late thirties, and then realized that the postponement would be permanent. Like one in five women of her age, and a higher percentage of her class, she found she was infertile. She regretted that the tapping on her typewriter keys had drowned out the ticking of the biological clock.

"Like any major life crisis – a loss, a failure, a divorce, a death – the baby-quest was so intense and personal and raw that it put you up against everything you had been before and who you would be after."

We know from Anne that her behavior, her choices, were the result of the media messages beamed to her. It is highly probable that Marie's decision to end 200 generations of her kind, is also the result of social conditioning. Britain's Family Policies Studies Center in 1995 reported projections that approximately 20 percent of British women born in the Sixties, Seventies and Eighties will remain childless. "Couples may be deciding that they cannot afford to have children or that the cost to the women in lost earnings is too high," the Center says. The part of the feminist movement that urged women onto the commercial treadmill as some men tried to escape from it, obscured the decrease in real income of Western workers, so that now a wife must usually work from *necessity* to maintain living standards.

Where have the fruits beyond necessity from Western workers' toil gone in the last half-century, when technology with cybernetics have vastly increased productivity? To feed the pigeons! (And the fat cats). Billions and billions – probably trillions worth of Western wealth has been transferred to other areas. But no clear public vote was ever held to decide it.

In 1991, professor William Graham of Ontario wrote, "There are areas of knowledge which have been wallpapered over with the products of communication – images and pseudo-realities. This subversion of education and knowledge has given rise to what Vaclav Havel, in *Letters to Olga*, called 'the crisis of human identity,' [though he probably means western identity]. Havel wrote from a Communist prison, 'All art and modern drama addresses the great theme of the 'crisis of human identity.' It is the central issue now facing the 'collective spirit' of humanity...the disintegration of man's oneness with himself and the loss of everything that gives human existence a meaningful order, continuity, and its unique outline.'"

The Communist prison has gone, but we live in a culture of compliance which reduces "the life of the mind to the content of media messages; and, in addition, fills the content of life with the ideal of becoming a consumer – first of all a consumer of the images, and thereafter a consumer of the products (pseudo-realities) illuminated by the images. Thus a human being comes to have a place only within the overall administrative institutional and economic plan" (*Advances in Information Systems Research*, 1991, Wm. Graham, Ontario Confederation of University Faculty Assns., *Human Consciousness, the Compliance Culture and Global Responsibility*, Windsor: Univ. of Windsor, 10-11.).

This is a form of pollution of values that the western establishment has transferred across political borders, climates, languages, customs. The many colors of Benetton. Big Mac. Coke adds Life: according to legend, a slogan translated into one African language as "Coke brings your ancestors back from the dead." An acquaintance who sought out the last traditional master weaver in a remote Nepalese village, found him in a small upper room. On the wall a poster – Madonna – an American performer.

In his foreword to the program of the first International Congress on Applied Systems Research and Cybernetics in Acapulco in 1980, Congress President, George Lasker, wrote of our world in which "the secondary values are so frequently being raised to absolute values, we have a special responsibility to ourselves and future generations..." to promote those values that optimize what we are.

Another participant in the 1980 conference noted that the Vatican had "reviewed the 347-year-old conviction of Galileo for supporting the heresy that the earth revolved around the sun with certain 'proofs.' But in the much younger biological sciences, we are still at a stage of suffering from established authorities and misperceptions of biological laws and 'proofs.' With Galileo or Galton, we must allow that there may be no absolute 'proofs:' the laws must often be inferred, and then continuously questioned and tested to bring them into more perfect accord with observation" (John, R. Applied System and Cybernetics, Lasker, G.E., ed. Pergamon, 1981, Vol. 1, 135).

Since then, we have had the consciousness-raising of the ecology movement and the issue of **Biodiversity.** The species that are alive today are less than one-tenth of 1 percent of the species that have ever lived, yet why are there 12,000 living species of butterfly? Presumably their differences fit into different ecological niches, with overlap of course.

In the world today, there are at least 1,500 clearly identifiable nations that do not want to be forced into cultures not their own. This may have values of which we are hardly aware.

There are neuronal patterns common to human species that provide schemata (Ger. *anlagen* – plans, arrangements) for order, giving rise to such evidence of commonalty as speech, adornment, dance and music, possibly archetypes and myths, that seem to be *ab origine* and not the result of diffusion. It is my theory that there are ranges of extension and expression of these schemata that are racial and cultural and individual. When a line becomes extinct – or indistinct – a potential for the future is lost.

"Each individual – no matter how great or obscure – is a product of, is shaped by, his or her background, experiences, opportunities, environment and times. No individual has any control over whether he or she will be born or not, or over the time, place, or circumstances of that birth – whether in primitive or prehistoric times or in modern America, whether into Western Civilization or into one of the non-Western cultures. No one has the slightest control over his or her genetic inheritance: the physical, mental, and emotional equipment with which the individual is endowed genetically. One has no control over the choice of one's race, ethnic background or sex. The child cannot choose his or her parents, family, socio-economic class level, initial religious training, or educational opportunities, facilities or teachers."

"Few of us depart very radically from the patterns and directions set for us by our backgrounds, families or environments. Even as adults one may have little or no control over one's natural energies or body chemistry that may affect personality, emotions, and general effectiveness" (Cole, Wayne S. You Can't Get there From Here—But I Did. The Society for History of American Foreign Relations. Newsletter. Vol. 23, No.3, Sept. 1992, 36). There is great media pressure to trade our identity.

But we can choose our future. Marie has made a choice. It used to be said that Jesuits believed that if they could teach boys from before the age of nine, they would have them for a lifetime. Indoctrination is part of all schooling. Marie has been subjected to indoctrination. We lost the last of the Mohicans. We nearly lost the buffalo and the condor in our lifetime. We can choose for the future. **We could lose ourselves.**

Should Marie the Celt and Star Fleet Officer O'Brien be made aware of this? The originator of the Star Trek series, Gene Roddenberry, wrote into it the 'prime directive,' that the temptation to interfere in other cultures and civilizations must be resisited: a sophisticated concept in keeping with ecological thinking.

When I was traveling from Miami to New York, the man beside me had bought a little Guatemalan Indian boy he was taking back to Iceland. This island near the Arctic Circle fascinates economists with a puzzle: how can so few people make so much from so little? They have a strong work ethic, respect for practical education, a powerful sense of national identity and the most ethnic homogeneity among the Scandinavian countries. The Icelander in the plane thought he was doing some sort of good, one supposes. We think it was a very selfish act, against the child and the people of Iceland. We need to rethink some of our activities and values, biological values. Nothing is more threatening to the survival of a species than the disappearance of naturally occurring genetic variations (Masters, R.D. (1990); Evolutionary Biology and Political Theory. *American Political Science Review*, vol. 84, No. 1, 195-210) yet interracial sexual and reproductive activity is promoted in the mass media as hyper exciting and socially desirable. That is a form of culture distortion, in which globalist media people use social "anti-matter" instead of creativity and life enhancing inspiration. People naturally take pride in perpetuating or developing what they are. Differentiation is part of the process of biological and cultural evolution.

For almost three decades, Star Trek fans invested money, time and imagination into the most successful dramatic television series of all time. Since Roddenberry's death, the Hollywood scriptwriters for another series – an extension of *Star Trek: The Next Generation, – Deep Space Nine,* married Chief Engineer O'Brien with his fruity Irish brogue – to an Oriental. Deanna Troi, a well-rounded ship's counselor-therapist, kisses and obviously has sexual intercourse with a "life form," Security Officer Worf, of clearly evident recent reptilian ancestry. Progeny from such unions must break the chain of ancestry of hundreds of generations of O'Briens and Trois. An Irish brogue could not have survived into the future unless there was a consciousness for preservation of identity, of ethnicity, of race, of species. These visual messages are false and therefore confusing. Children who watch them should be de-programmed in their biology classes.

The marketing media in the western world, destructive of the principle of preservation of biodiversity and following equalist dogma, gives another false message. In the United States and abroad, the series has become the most successful syndication

What would be the next 'Next Generation'?

Engineering Officer Miles O'Brien in the 24th century speaks with an Irish brogue and looks the Irish Colin Meaney he is. Such an ethnic identity could only have persisted had there been an understanding of the value of the continuity of species and sub-species diversity. Yet, in the spin-off *Deep Space Nine*, scriptwriters married him to a Japanese "ethnobotanist," who gives birth to their child. Result: end of millennia of development of the parents' biodiversity; for the child, a conflict or confusion of identification.

Deanna Troi, *Enterprise* counselor-therapist, seems to have been at one time "in love" with fellow-human but not empath, Will Riker. The more in common, the more likely is love to last. But it includes sexual desire and for her, the desire for Riker has gone. Isolated by her special gift, she is drawn to another isolate and one-of-a-kind on the *Enterprise*, Worf, a Klingon raised by humans. Unlike the Beauty and the Beast story, there is no prince. Troi's object cannot change into the image of her wishes.

Security Officer Worf's appearance portrays the large reptilian component persisting from his ancestry. With this, scriptwriters project the appropriate compassionless, rigid, fight-to-the death personality. Yet with the perversity which is common in our society, and propinquity, Troi encourages him to be her sexual partner, and projects upon him certain of her feelings that are not part of his genetic inheritance; just as lawyers have been known to "fall in love" with a client killer sociopath, someone without empathy, a heritable personality deficit almost inconceivable to a normal person.

venture in television history. A message that is part of many of these episodes is one of ending human ethnic and species biodiversity through hybridization. The writers and producers of this type of material do more than subvert our culture, they tend to distort and destroy our peoples' futures. The sign that was once posted in the main reception area of the main line advertising agency, N.W. Ayer, read: *We create your wants. We create your desires* (Shorris, 1994)), has been made true.

But in the film *Star Trek: Generations*, produced at the end of the television series, the exemplary character of Captain Jean-Luc Picard is strengthened by the portrayal of his deep cognitive and affective regard for family ethnic and territorial continuity. His basic life assumption has been that while he devoted his life to Star Fleet, in his words "the family would go on" through his nephew. The Picard family, tending their vineyards in France would continue as they had for millennia. This dependency upon the connecting link of a single collateral descendant is tenuous. In the film, Picard receives news of the accidental deaths of his brother and nephew. It is his greatest life crisis, expunging an assumption upon which so many decisions had rested; a potentially devastating crisis of end of identity. Akin to the temptations of Christ or St. Anthony, Picard is tempted with a fantasy of the joy and happiness of the family he never had.

We must raise the consciousness of peoples that the destruction of their identities is a worse fate for mankind and their kind than all the other ecological disasters of Man.

Whatever our race, five millennia from Otzi the Celt, we can go into museums and see the works of our ancestors. We can commune with the arts of the centuries up to our own. In another century, will that still be possible for the majority of Mankind?

Understanding of social-biological realities should give new upbeat insights to artists and writers, support decisions toward the continuation of the spotted owl in primal forests of the American Northwest, of the snail-darter fish, and of Celts like ice-man Otzi and Marie. For 12,000 species of butterfly to survive, and for 1,500 nations to flourish, we must make conscious an evolutionary way of thinking, so as to resist and reject with reason the subversions of our lives and future by invisible oligarchic transnationals served by "bloodless" bureaucrats, by "Bennetons" and the other equalists, .

Sociobiology demonstrates how, by helping your kin, you are also helping your genes: this is called *kin altruism* or *kin selection*. Your personal survival only matters insofar as it promotes the successful replication of your genes. You do not even have to have children; your nieces and nephews have as many of your genes as would your grandchildren. People in their wills leave most of their property to relatives, rather than friends, resources that increase their kin's reproductive potential. And, at another systems level, when a white billionaire offered to fund a course on Western civilization at Yale University, it would have enhanced the probability of the continuation of Western civilization and Western genes. People of non-European origin who opposed acceptance of the grant were unconsciously rejecting such a weighting different from *their* competing present-future continuum.

To understand is to begin to change, and to choose instead of confusion, a new enlightenment of free review of data of difference and to expose regression toward a new Middle Age of superstition and self-doubt.

What we should recognize as "sacred" is not human life, for that may be given up altruistically or forfeited as punishment; what should be sacred is the continuity of life, human or other, along its traditional lines of development. "Integration" is disintegration.

"Any path which narrows future possibilities may become a lethal trap. Humans are not threading their way through a maze; they scan a vast horizon filled with unique opportunities. The narrowing viewpoint of the maze should appeal only to creatures with their noses buried in sand. Sexually produced uniqueness and differences are the life-protection of the species."—The Spacing Guild Handbook, in *Children of Dune* by Frank Herbert.

Should Marie and Star Fleet Officer O'Brien and their spouses have been made aware of this?

If your answer is Yes, then one should understand the sociobiological imperative or systems dynamic underlying the question: What is my obligation to make others aware of this? Clue - Genes!

Centuries have passed since Peter Abelard (1079-1142) contended with Bernard of Clairvaux for the primacy of reason and wrote to him offering the great theme – *diversa non adversa.* Can we use this wisdom now? Diversity should no longer imply enmity. Diversity deserves respect, understanding and support, for it is a part of the pattern of life. Can we agree with an early vice-president of India, S. Radhakrishnan, who wrote supporting variety of ways of life and diversity of peoples, "But they should all be covered or sublimated by the perception of the unity which underlies the whole of the diversity." And if we agree, shall we so act?

In preparing this exposition, I found in my notebooks Edmund Burke's conception of **society as a partnership "between those who are living, those who are dead, and those who are to be born."**
On the same page were two other quotations: "He who would move the earth must first move himself." *Aristotle?* And,

What Am I Doing Here?

**I believe in putting into life at least as much
as one has taken out.**

**I respect the devotion of those who have preserved
for me the precious heritage of the past.
Without its stored wealth I would start with nothing.**

**I believe in the sacredness of duty to conserve
and renew our heritage and to preserve it
for my descendants.**

**I believe in the challenge of the future,
realizing that its existence depends upon me.**

— Robert John

We have reached a new level of understanding of the movement from chaos to order of which we – and all that we think and do are a part – from the chaos of exploding stars to the order of elements, the order of repeatable interactions, the order of muscles and movement, the order of thought and sounds - speech and music, and other arts and behaviors.
Just as in the early 20th century the path of an electron was first seen in a cloud chamber, so at its end, we can see a New Enlightenment capability for a meta and systems understanding of human and animal behaviors, and plant and natural phenomena interactions. We can continue the separation of what is mere superstition and the flotsam and jetsam of development from wisdom.
If James Hervey Johnson of San Diego were to read this first book, I and all who really knew him know he would feel vindicated and pleased. It may help to continue some of his genes – and yours!
— Malcom Dalgliesh.